P9-BJU-315

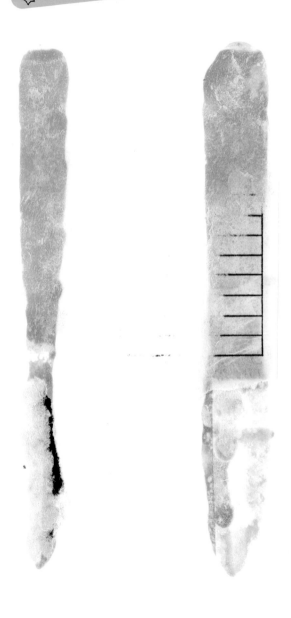

PETER KOESTENBAUM is Professor of Philosophy at San Jose State University. He has received the statewide Outstanding Professor Award of the California State University and Colleges and is an associate director of the Psychological Studies Institute of Palo Alto, California. His other books include *Managing Anxiety: The Power of Knowing Who You Are* and *The Vitality of Death: Essays in Existential Psychology and Philosophy.*

SPECTRUM BOOKS IN HUMANISTIC PSYCHOLOGY,

edited by Rollo May and Charles Hampden-Turner, aim to present those psychological viewpoints that place the human being at the organizing center of social reality. It assumes that persons have potential for growth and unfolding in relationship with others, that the ideas they hold about themselves have important consequences, at least partly self-fulfilling. Human beings are free to choose, yet choices once made have determinable, and sometimes inexorable, results, for which the social scientist must share responsibility. In short, we posit an unbreakable relationship between the knower and the known to which each contributes.

We present this series in the hope that a science of the human being will evolve which is worthy of the humanistic tradition and the richness of human endowments.

Rollo May

Charles Hampden-Turner

General Editors

Existential Sexuality

Choosing to Love

Peter Koestenbaum

Prentice-Hall, Inc. *Englewood Cliffs, New Jersey*

A SPECTRUM BOOK

Library of Congress Cataloging in Publication Data

KOESTENBAUM, PETER.
    Existential sexuality

    1. Sex.   2. Love.   3. Family.   I. Title.
[DNLM: 1. Existentialism.   2. Love.   3. Sex behavior.   HQ21 K78e   1974]
HQ21.K68   301.41   74-8385
ISBN 0-13-294934-2
ISBN 0-13-294926-1 (pbk.)

Special thanks are due to Mike Hunter, Betty Neville, and Jean Homan
for their support, acumen, and assistance in the preparation of this book.

Quotation from an article appearing in the *Jewish Community News*
is used by kind permission of the Jewish Federation of Greater San Jose.

The names, places, and identifying circumstances of the illustrative materials
in this book have been changed to protect the anonymity of my students.

PRENTICE-HALL INTERNATIONAL, INC. (*London*)

PRENTICE-HALL OF AUSTRALIA PTY. LTD. (*Sydney*)

PRENTICE-HALL OF CANADA LTD. (*Toronto*)

PRENTICE-HALL OF INDIA PRIVATE LIMITED (*New Delhi*)

PRENTICE-HALL OF JAPAN, INC. (*Tokyo*)

This book is dedicated to my private students in philosophy

Contents

PART THREE: FAMILY

Behold a good doctrine has been given you, forsake it not.

Proverbs 4:2

Introduction

WHAT IS EXISTENTIAL SEXUALITY?

Existential Sexuality is a comprehensive statement about how you can apply the insights of existential psychotherapy and existential philosophy to human loving relationships. This ranges from the free choice of one's sexuality, through the meaning of existential love and its representation in sex and intimacy, to the relevance of these insights to the life of the family. Throughout there are illustrations of how these ideas can help you answer such diverse practical questions as how to find more satisfaction in sex, how to manage a successful life without sex, how to distinguish love from sex, how to raise children, how to define your marriage, and even how to live with sexual aberrations.

Although the analyses and conclusions of *Existential Sexuality* are based on the existential-phenomenological personality theory, a detailed exposition of that theory is not needed to understand this book.* Nevertheless, and for purposes of reference, the master table of my existential personality theory is included as an appendix to this book. The master table is a succinct summary of what I consider to be the principal answers of existentialism and phenomenology to the question of how we can as human beings achieve the fulfillment of our potential.

* A more detailed analysis of that theory, together with tests to measure your authenticity, can be found in my book *Managing Anxiety* (Englewood Cliffs, N.J.: Prentice-Hall, Inc., 1974). A comprehensive statement of the existential personality theory and its phenomenological foundations is found in my book *The Vitality of Death* (Westport, Conn.: Greenwood Publishing Co., 1971).

1

Briefly stated, the existential personality theory maintains that man is first a freedom; he therefore chooses the respective meanings that love, sex, marriage, and children are to have in his life. There are, obviously, many choices available, but the authentic choice, which I recommend, is one that is harmonious with the ego-world field of consciousness that is man. The structure of that field is described by the master table.* Although we are free to choose against love, if we do choose for it, certain patterns are more in keeping with the philosophically disclosed nature of man than are others. I call that decision for harmony with nature "existential love" or "existential sexuality." If you choose existential love, then you begin by understanding and creating a love relationship. Only later do you translate this love into physical, that is, sexual, expression. That sequence is but one possible option, it is neither a logical nor a physical requirement.

* See Appendix A.

I

How to Choose
Your Kind of Sex

FREEDOM

Human beings are not by nature sexual, as Freud and his followers have contended, but choose to be so. Sex is a natural urge, but the role it plays in your life and the importance you attribute to it—your attitude toward your sexual urge—is a matter of free choice. The four fundamental elements in your love life are sex, love, marriage, and children. There is no logical connection between them. Each of these four elements exists independently as either a biological fact, a psychological fact, or a social institution. You are free to choose any, all, or none as part of your project of creating meaning in your life. You are also free to define the relationships that are to exist for you among these four elements. For example, whether or not love is to precede sex, whether or not sex demands love, and whether or not either love or sex are the true foundations for a marriage, are all questions which have no objective or expert answer but must be resolved by your own free powers of self-definition. An authentic and liberated person can take charge of that important act of self-definition in his life, and he is thereby the "master of his fate."

The conjunction of these four elements may in fact be incorporated into our social institutions, religious views, anthropological theories, and the history of mankind. However, from the points of view of both logic and the nature of man, these four elements are not connected in any necessary way. Specifically, love and sex are not joined with any kind of compulsion; however, they can be joined beautifully and produce ideal, or existential, sex. The conjunction of love and sex is a fulfilling experience—if it can be worked out. But the myth that this conjunction is normal to the nature of man is so dangerous that it has destroyed countless marriages, dismembered families, and disrupted promising and meaningful interpersonal relationships.

Man's freedom is both his heaven and his hell, both his salvation and his perdition. You are free to distinguish love from marriage. That is a saving insight if you have a bad marriage. You are equally free to identify love and sex with one another. That possibility opens to you one of the great experiences of mankind. To be free means to be an adult. But how many of us are ready to be adults?

Many people conceptualize their dissatisfaction with life in terms of sexual problems, but their real difficulty lies in misunderstanding the role of sex in life. As a rule, they feel that the meaning of sex in life is fixed, when in fact it is constantly developing and changing—it is free. That simple insight, when integrated fully into the lifestyle of an individual, can liberate him from the chains of his pain.

THREE WOMEN

Following are three letters from women who, for different reasons, are dissatisfied with their sexual experiences. Rhoda is promiscuous and does not really enjoy sex, whereas Ruth is promiscuous and does not enjoy marriage. Stephanie refuses all sex and is reasonably happy but feels guilty. All three have one common complaint: Each is unhappy sexually.

The real reason for their dissatisfaction is simple: Each misunderstands the role of sex in life. The problem for Rhoda and Ruth is the fragmentation of sex. Both expect sex to have *meaning* (rather than pleasure) by itself. In fact, however, it has meaning only in connection with love. Sex without love can give *pleasure,* like a delicious piece of candy eaten in a hurry. But meaning is something else. Meaning stands for integration; meaning refers to a total life and to the fulfillment of its potential. Both Rhoda and Ruth want ideal sex but search for it as if it were an isolated physical pleasure rather than a total being-experience. Rhoda and Ruth believe that improved sexual techniques will insure a meaningful life; but ideal sex, existential or meaningful sex, is sex experienced as an integral part of a beautiful life. There is a difference. Furthermore, existential *sex* is a total, integral experience, one which is built on a foundation of existential *love.* In subsequent chapters I will define and describe existential love and its integration with sexuality to bring about the larger phenomenon of existential sex.

Stephanie's case is different. She is unable to distinguish sex from love, and as a result she cannot experience love. She has been taught that only through sex can love be experienced and expressed, and yet she wants love without sex. Her guilt, based on the misconception that love and sex are forever welded together, prevents her from loving and being loved. And that is a pity; hers is a wasted life.

The three letters that follow illustrate the depth of confusion between love and sex. They also suggest the power we all have to define our own attitude to this complex.

Rhoda

I have been drinking tonight; quite heavily as a matter of fact, and I guess it must take a real loosening up like this to make me realize I have a problem.

Dr. Koestenbaum, I am afraid of myself. I'm worried about my future. I am a very headstrong and selfish person; yet I also believe I am sensitive to others and can be quite compassionate. But within the last year or two I think I've begun to go off on a track that will eventually lead to disaster. I believe the core of my problem is sex. I am torn between the desire to stay single, maintain my unique individuality, and remain independent, and the extreme need I have for security and companionship, and even more especially for sexual fulfillment. I am only 21 and I am sure I have had intimate sexual experiences with far more than the average amount of men for my age. I started late but I have had a very busy sex life. The problem is, I am never satisfied. I have reached orgasm only three times in my life by actual male stimulation (although I am able to stimulate myself successfully) and it seems that I am madly in search of the ultimate orgasm. I jump from bed to bed, and from one noncommittal relationship to the next. When I fall in love with the man I am quite devoted until either I become frustrated at my lack of response or I recoil from my partner's possessiveness. Lately, I have turned more and more to men whom I know to be dedicated bachelors at present, which frustrates me even more, because I want the security of being loved.

I cannot find love or sexual gratification and I'm worried about what my current behavior is doing to my personality, and my future. I am becoming increasingly cynical and my relationships less close all the time, yet I am not strong enough to sit home alone and wait for the right person. I don't feel guilty about sex and I do enjoy it, but I seem to have forgotten how to start a relationship that is not based solely on the physical aspects.

I feel this may be more of a common problem for young women in this age of free morality than many would like to admit.

I'm alone tonight; tired, lonely, frustrated and unhappy, and tho' I will more than likely lose this mood after a good night's sleep, I feel that these inner feelings have been painfully exposed through the indulgence of alcohol, and that they are my true feelings, and they are problems that do need very definite solutions before I try to hide them tomorrow behind my façade of modern young liberated woman.

I will be grateful for your help.

Sincerely,
Rhoda

Ruth

When my husband and I first married we had agreed that whatever type of involvement one of us wanted we should not feel limited by the other's desires—we should consider them and then act according to our own decisions. Fine—until after five years of marriage and a two-year-old son I began a heady involvement with a male friend. For four months we spent a great deal of our time together—working, studying, talking, and so on together. At the end of the spring semester we were very good buddies and we split without overt sexual involvement. . . .

After a month, I saw him again. He had missed me and told me he loved me and although I knew his feelings must be similar to mine—I did not define my feelings as love. But our relationship became sexual at that point. Because my husband and I had pledged complete honesty to one another, I kept him accurately informed of everything. He was aware that I liked this man very much and had expressed some discomfort since I was adamant that no sexuality was to be involved . . . and later it did become involved. At that point things began to disintegrate. My husband believed this man, whom he had met several times, was manipulating me—and I was to cut off all relationships with him.

Long, heavy encounters began—my assertion that this was contrary to the way things should be according to me and to the way I had assumed my husband believed they should be as well . . . his assertion that at the "gut level" he could not stand the knowledge of my sexuality with another man.

He decided that if I wanted to continue the relationship I would have to immediately go to work and support 50% of the household expenses, etc., etc. And even this would not "pacify" him. He could not continue our husband-wife relationship as it was.

I decided that perhaps with my responsibility to my child and to the six in-laws with whom we live and who are without their own means of support, I should not assert my desires so ultimately and agreed to continue the relationship on a non-sexual basis (no touching, kissing, etc.). But I was angry and uncomfortable with myself and with my husband. . . .

Then, my husband decided that I should not continue the relationship at all. Things became violently aggressive—and finally ended in a fight where my husband struck me in the face and I told him that I refused to live any longer under his domination, and I would leave.

At this point we both acknowledged that there had to be another way to communicate and to relate.

Now, we have stayed together trying to build a relationship which is comfortable to both of us. But his obvious desire is that I should spend every moment of my life joining his. I should play with him—learn with him—love with him only only only. I feel stifled.

He has a concept of super-dedicated, idealized, total union with me. I don't want that intensity—that responsibility in the relationship. Yet I do want a relationship with my husband. . . .

I am continuing the relationship with my friend on a sexual (not intercourse) basis and look forward to being with him again in the fall. Things at home are not comfortable in the sense that in every quiet moment with my husband there is tension present by his insistence on my telling him every detail of my day and my thoughts. I feel like he is too encroaching . . . that I have no separation from him . . . that he is forcing me to live by his decisions by making it so uncomfortable for me to tell him things which he might dislike.

Now, when I am so involved with existential thoughts, things really seem to be beyond my control. There is no way out of this dilemma and I have decided to just do as much as I can and then become apathetic to my own desires.

Sincerely,
Ruth

Stephanie

I am a woman who is forty-years old and on the surface very happily married. I have never consulted with anyone on my personal problems, but you inspire confidence and your non-medical and non-psychological approach—your philosophy—sounds very promising to me. My husband, who is fifty-two, is devoted and a well-known lawyer in this community (a corporation specialist) and he makes a great deal of money. Yet I feel constricted all over and frustrated all the time. I am tense, my stomach muscles are always tight, and I have dizzy spells. My internist can find no physical cause for them.

My principal symptom is that I am constantly on the verge of tears and I find that very embarrassing. I never cry hard. But when my tears begin to flow and my eyes redden I get tight in the stomach, tight in the neck, and even my facial muscles feel taut and constricted. I have tried to sob—even to sob in fantasy, as you have suggested in your lectures—but I cannot bring myself to do that.

I know I dream actively but I cannot ever remember or describe my dreams.

My friends tell me I am too timid and coy—too obedient and eager to please. I do remember my mother spanking me for crying as a child. Perhaps I'm still fearful.

I have six children. I love them, but I cannot express my love to them. My relationship with them is formal and perfunctory and stiff. I love to sing. I have a good voice, I use it.

I must confide in you something over which I am deeply ashamed and that no one knows except my husband. I have no sex life. I never had much—I never wanted any—we've had no sex since the birth of our last daughter eight years ago. I don't want sex; I don't need sex. I love my husband very much but I feel terrible guilt. He must resent me deeply, hate me. I know he has no other women. I am a failure. Are there men who can love without sex? Have you in your counseling experience met any?

I would rather be left alone. You know, Dr. Koestenbaum, I did have a fantasy about my ideal life, as you suggested in class. The most comforting fantasy that I have—and it pains me to admit it—is to think of my husband having died: Then I have no guilt feelings about depriving him of sex.

I would like to change, Dr. Koestenbaum. I hate housework, I hate cooking and I hate having sex with my husband. I would like to change so I could learn to like these things.

I would be very much interested in your comments and so would my husband.

Thank you,
Stephanie

ANALYSIS

A simplified analysis of these letters yields the following insights: (1) Their so-called problems are based on the assumption that there is a right and proper form of sexual behavior; (2) they have repressed knowledge and understanding of their freedom to connect or sever, identify, or dissociate the various aspects of love, sex, marriage, and the family; and (3) they are unaware of their freedom to define themselves within the general biological and social structures with which they find themselves. If they can be made aware of this freedom, then all three women will become transformed personalities.

Rhoda wants love and seeks it through sex. She is easily available sexually; but she does not want sex for its own sake. She wants love. Somewhere in her education she has been misled by our culture and its insidious materialism to believe that physical manipulation leads to an intimacy of consciousnesses or to spiritual fulfillment; she has been taught that sex leads to love. Her sexual experiences are unsatisfactory not because she uses poor techniques or because she feels guilt or anything of the sort. The meaning of Rhoda's intended statement "I no longer enjoy sex" (or "I enjoy sex with serious qualifications.") is, in translation, "I want love but do not have it." The search for love is a philosophical enterprise, whereas the search for sex is a psychological, physiological, and biological activity. Her culture has not taught her how to be a consciousness, nor has it taught her how to encounter another consciousness. She searches for love like an impotent husband who expresses love towards his wife by hiring a man to impregnate her!

Rhoda wants love to be expressed in sex. This connection is a human possibility that can be chosen freely. (There are circumstances in life, however, in which a person's sanity can be maintained by the philosophic knowledge that *it is just as authentic to choose love without sex*.) Rhoda *wants* to choose love combined with sex but she does not know how to go about it. And that lack of knowledge comes down to ignorance about the structure of her inward consciousness, about the nature of a human encounter in the intersubjective intimacy of love, and about the secrets of expressing the nature of consciousness and intimacy in the flesh of sexuality. This book is intended to help her and everyone with such problems. Rhoda needs to acquire an authentic consciousness of her own and then to develop an authentic relationship with another mature adult consciousness. Finally, to be fulfilled sexually, Rhoda and her mature lover must make the decision to translate their encounter into sexuality. Rhoda has to understand what existential love is and *then* she has to learn how to integrate existential love into a total existential sexual experience.

Ruth uses her sexuality to punish her husband. This is a neurotic use of sex. Ruth has not *chosen* her lifestyle; she has not assumed *personal responsibility* for the definition of her sexuality. She must say to herself: "I define myself as a woman who uses sex to punish her man. I assume full responsibility for that self-definition because I have decided that it is *right* to punish my man." Then there is no problem associated with her behavior—if she continues to make that choice.

In addition, Ruth has redefined the marriage contract to include total permissiveness for herself. Again, there is nothing intrinsically wrong with that redefinition. She thinks promiscuity is right or natural and that her husband is unfair in not recognizing it. The fact is that promiscuity is defined and chosen by Ruth as right. She is entitled to that choice.

However in choosing promiscuity she is choosing also the consequences. Ruth ignores the truth that freedom can be experienced only when translated into action. And once that is done, the actions turn into consequences. Consequences are the children of our freedom. A person who is free must also identify himself with the consequences of that freedom. Rhoda has neglected to recognize this existential truism. She might choose more pleasing consequences—such as a husband who will agree with her definition of the marriage contract, or no husband at all —unless she wishes to choose conflict as part of her total lifestyle.

Finally, Stephanie suffers needlessly from guilt because society—with its ghost-in-a-machine theory of man, which is a materialistic and mechanical personality theory (the position that human beings are things and not persons, objects rather than subjectivities)—has brainwashed her into thinking that conjugal love can be expressed only through sex. She wants inner integrity, maturity, and authenticity, and she expresses this desire through yoga and devotion to her large family. She does not know that sex and love are different and can be separated. Believing they must be one, she perceives of herself as a failure. Her entire world is thus a "failure"; she is frequently depressed and is therefore depressing to those around her. Stephanie must learn that love without sex is a totally authentic possibility. She can choose that lifestyle with a clear conscience. She might thereby contravene the canons of society, but she is most certainly not violating human nature by exercising her freedom in this way.

EXISTENTIAL SEX IS A CHOICE AND NOT A NEED

This chapter examines the cluster of decisions that *precede* an ideal love relationship, sexual relationship, marriage relationship, and parent-child relationship. Subsequent chapters will explore the nature of existential love as the encounter of two freedoms. Only after existential *love* is understood can one work on an ideal *sexual* relationship and establish what I call existential sex.

The decision preceding existential sex is the choice of integration rather than fragmentation as a lifestyle. That choice is not an absolute one. The ascetic chooses fragmentation; so does the stoic, the person who lives by will power, reason, and adherence to duty. These are legitimate and authentic choices. They follow directly from the one fundamental rule of human existence: I am freedom (principle C7 on the master table). The choice of existential sex, however, is the decision to combine the spiritual and biological possibilities of human existence into a single "field-of-consciousness" experience.*

The preexistential notion was that all men and women had predestined sexual natures and roles. Lord Byron expressed that view: "Man's love is of man's life a thing apart;/'Tis woman's whole existence," he wrote. The existential view is that such an absolute distinction between men and women is chosen, and can be changed.

What is existential sex? Existential sex is chosen sex; it is the sex life that an individual has chosen authentically.† Love can be expressed through the body to a member of the opposite sex. But love can also be expressed to God only (or in a more abstract sense, as with yoga). The latter can be as authentic an expression of love as heterosexuality. It is also quite possible to relinquish love altogether as an ideal. There is no law that says life must include love. Neither does a law exist that says sex must express love. Our freedom is total.

In fact, infinite possibilities exist. To know that is to be free and unburdened. Marriage and sex manuals are dangerous—they imply that "normal" people either in fact do live according to the manual's principles, or at least strive to live in that fashion, *because they must.* Marriage manuals have an insidious and inauthentic message. They say, in effect, "I am the truth about man. If you live according to my precepts you live right. If you violate these rules then you live wrong; you are then defective and must feel inadequate. You can allay your guilt by following the procedures in this book."

This dogmatic approach forces conformity to artificial and dehumanizing models. The truth about man is his freedom. His freedom, which is his essence, means that no one self-definition is the only truth.

The Decision to Cope

To choose ideal love as the meaning of life is to build on previous choices, all of which are equally free. What are these choices?

---

* The field-of-consciousness theory of man is the view that human beings are zones of subjectivity and consciousness, which include their bodies, rather than purely biological specimens. Man is a spiritual nature in addition to his body.

The field-of-consciousness theory is developed in detail in my book *Managing Anxiety* (Englewood Cliffs, N.J.: Prentice-Hall, Inc., 1974).

† To operate authentically is to express in one's life the principles of the master table.

The first decision is, "Do I choose to cope with the sexual aspect of my life or do I choose not to cope with this aspect?" Think about it for a while. Remember that you have already made some choice and that you are now living that choice. But you may also have chosen to forget the choice which you have in fact made and which you are now living. Think again. Have you chosen to cope? Or have you chosen to give up? Do you like the choice you have been living?

The decision to cope, as a central choice, far transcends decisions about sex in importance.

In August of 1972, the Democratic Presidential candidate, Senator George McGovern, met the great test of his mettle. Senator Eagleton, his chosen running-mate, was discovered to have had a history of mental illness, treatment for which included electroconvulsive therapy. McGovern had to choose between (a) retaining and (b) dropping his running-mate a week after the Democratic National Convention had nominated them both. The big decision which confronted McGovern was *not* "shall I drop Eagleton?" It was "shall I cope with this crisis or shall I give up?" If McGovern decides to cope he shows that decision by remaining calm, detached, rational and tough. Should he decide to give up he will show that by contradicting himself, being nervous and irritable and, as a last resort, resigning from the ticket himself. McGovern did choose to cope.

Now ask yourself these questions: "When was my last major crisis?" Remember it and relive it in detail. "What was my actual choice, as expressed in my actions and behavior?" "Did I choose to cope or did I choose not to cope?" And finally, "What can I learn from this experience?"

But let us return to human sexuality. What are the symptoms of having chosen to cope? They are energy, joy, control, security, peace, and confidence. If that is how you feel about sex—whether you are sexually active or not—then you have chosen to cope with the sexual aspects of your life.

If, on the other hand, sex makes you feel guilty, depressed, inadequate, insecure, in conflict, and drained of energy, you probably have chosen not to cope with the sexual aspect of your life. No one can be sure by how you live and what you do whether or not you have chosen to cope. You can tell only by the way you yourself feel.

Bernice

Bernice, for example, freely chose to cope with a series of unhappy love affairs and family debacles by giving up sex altogether, like a nun. For Bernice, that was authentic coping. Once she chose to end involvement with men and reorganized her life accordingly, she felt a sense of relief, relaxation, and joy. What made Bernice's coping authentic was that she chose it authentically. True, social pressures and images were constantly in the background and had to be fought. Society does not respect an individual's integrity, individuality, and uniqueness. The message of society is still tribal: conform or be ostracized. Fortunately, our society is becoming increasingly enlightened. Bernice was able to surround herself with adult human beings who supported her authentic choices, who respected her decisions.

She could also have chosen sexual promiscuity authentically. In that case, a different cluster of social pressures would have descended upon her. She would then have been called upon to seek support from different sections of society. But Bernice did not choose this latter option. In other words, the form of the choice and not the content is what makes it authentic coping. Choosing to cope is the iron will never to accept defeat.

Bernice's twin sister, Marguerite, hoped to avoid what she felt were Bernice's neurotic shortcomings. Marguerite followed so-called "common" or "traditional" views on sex, love, marriage, and children. In other words, Marguerite was brainwashed into believing that a woman, to be "normal," must have a sex life, a husband, and children. In fact, she was sexually promiscuous, married early, had children early, and continued her promiscuity. However, Marguerite was never happy, satisfied, or at peace with herself. Lately, she has taken to alcohol and pills, which she gets legally by feigning migraine headaches and moving from physician to physician to insure she will continue to receive them. She has already turned to prostitution.

Why? The source of Marguerite's troubles is not her sexual activities —any more than Bernice's sexual abstinence is the source of her joy. Marguerite's troubles are symptoms of inauthentic coping, of the choice not to cope with her life-situation. Blaming sex or men is escaping her responsibility for coping. Intense sexual desire is her rationalized excuse for choosing not to cope.

Now ask yourself again, as you take stock of your sex life, whether or not you have chosen to cope. Rather than reflecting on a past crisis, consider how ready you are to take on new crises. A crisis comes; how do you react? With panic? Do you become childish? Are you later ashamed of how you responded? Start again: The crisis comes. Before you react, ask yourself loud and clear: Do I choose to cope or do I choose not to cope?

If you were a noncoping person and you now choose to cope, then you have chosen to redefine yourself as a new person. You will discover the miraculous power of your freedom. You will discover that coping is easy, possible, workable, and rewarding. There can be no situation which is beyond coping—if you have chosen to define yourself as a person who copes. That is how business executives and politicians, administrators and generals, successfully manage situations of impossible stress. And that is how patients grow in existential psychotherapy.

Authentic Choice

Let us now return to the choice of existential sex. Your life is as it is: Some of it is good and some of it is bad. You are now living with the decisions of your past, some of which turned out to have been wise and others to have been mistakes. Let us take a look at what may be a typical college student. Specifically, he experiences a conflict. He has been taught by the culture that sex is a key part of the meaning of life. Movies, novels, magazines, sex manuals, some behavioral scientists and friends have conspired to brainwash him into believing that life is sex. In addition, the stark realities of life have created for him a situation in which ideal sex just does not exist and he sees no way to bring it about. It is this dilemma that existentialism must solve. Now he must speak honestly to himself: "Given these facts, do I choose to cope with life as it exists for me or do I choose not to cope with it?" To choose to cope is to choose contact with reality. To choose not to cope is to choose alienation from reality and escape into fantasy.

The principal lesson to be learned is that we must constantly be on the alert for two things: First, we must always be *aware* of the choices which we actually do make regarding coping. It is good practice to examine each act and each thought with the question, "Am I now choosing to cope or am I now choosing not to cope?" The answer is usually obvious. Second, we must *practice* continuously choosing to cope. This can be accomplished by simply being awake to each situation. Again, you must tell yourself—even if for only a few minutes at a stretch—"I am now choosing to cope with life." Soon that theme will dominate all moments of your life.

If you now choose to cope, if you take charge of your life, you will be able to make the following decision authentically: "Do I choose to search for ideal or existential sex or do I choose not to search for ideal sex?" That is one of the great decisions of your life. Life does not tell you how to choose. Experts do not exist who can tell you which choice is right. It is the deliberate freedom of your decision which makes the disposition of the dilemma either authentic or inauthentic. The decision is based on subjective free choice and not on some objective, absolute value system.

Let me outline the criteria of authentic choice: (1) It is a decision made by you, with a minimum of external influences. Those external factors that do influence you are chosen by you, are admitted by your free choice. (2) It is a decision made deliberately and not unconsciously. It is a decision that you clearly know you made, so that you are prepared to assume full responsibility for it. (3) It is a decision based on maximum philosophical and personal self-disclosure. That is to say, it is a decision based on an understanding of the nature of man (philosophical self-disclosure) and a meaningful overview of the kind of person that you individually and uniquely are (personal self-disclosure). (See point B on the master table.) (4) It is a decision which "feels" right, which brings relief rather than burdens, joy rather than guilt, and a sense of freedom rather than of slavery.

2
Existential Love
For Adults Only

The questions, "What is love?" "How must I live to be in love and to be worthy of being loved?" "What can I do to bring love into my life?" have always been with us. What is the existential prescription for success and meaning in this important aspect of our lives?

ADULTHOOD

You can choose love; you do not have to. Existential love is possible only for the mature, authentic individual. This is the *first* theme of existential love. To the extent that an individual has fulfilled the criteria of the master table he is able to experience authentic love or encounter. There exist no simple techniques for love. In fact, to love through techniques is itself a manifestation of inauthenticity. If you are mature, that is, philosophically and personally self-disclosed and have integrated the insights of the master table into your life, you are ready for love. If you are lucky, love will also choose you.

When a young man, a student, asks me, "Professor, I'm lonely; how can I find a girl?" I answer, "Grow up!" I then add, "In your present state of development it is easier to grow up than to search for a girl. Work on yourself, not on others. As you continue to grow up, the kind of relationships you then desire will appear of their own accord." It is indeed reassuring to all frustrated young people to know that self-improvement leads to love, since self-improvement is possible and even easy, while searching directly for love is an illusion and never works.

Consequences

Six important practical consequences follow from the fact that love is only for the mature. These consequences can make most individuals relaxed, happy, and filled with hope.

First, the romantic period of life is closer to the middle than to the beginning of life. In the teens and early twenties, the body is young, the glands active, and energy is abundant. Because we are a culture focused on things and objects (the ghost-in-the-machine theory of man) rather than on awareness, consciousness, and inwardness (the field-of-consciousness theory of man), we believe that it is the bodily, organic, and physiological conditions associated with youth that bring about love. But that is not true. The young glands may bring about frequent copulation and speedy pregnancy, but these events are not to be confused with love. It takes an independent act based on maturity and authenticity to connect copulation and pregnancy with the phenomenon of love. In actual fact, copulation and pregnancy are often the opposite of love: They can be an escape from home, from growing up, and, in general, from facing the implacable but beautiful realities of life itself.

Middle age, on the other hand, is a period in life where maturity and authenticity are more likely to exist than at an earlier stage of personal development. Of course, age per se is no guarantee of authenticity. Authenticity results from experience, decisions, commitments, courage, time, patience, and hard work. Thus, it would help all people to restructure our culture in order to emphasize the romantic possibilities of the postyouth period of life. Needed is a change in attitudes and self-image. The media for the public definition of human beings—magazines, movies, advertisers, clothiers, and the like—have the responsibility of portraying the possibilities for love as a futurized, hopeful, and mature experience rather than as a phenomenon that is past before it is real. Mature people and authentic individuals are far better lovers—in every sense of that word—than are the immature and inauthentic.

Second, marriage should be postponed as long as possible. Each individual must resolve to postpone marriage until he is assured of his own and his partner's authenticity. In many young marriages, the wedding is an escape from the responsibilities of authenticity. The wedding often means, in fact, "the burdens of growing up are too severe for me, let me therefore get married. Marriage means either automatic authenticity—a ceremony will bring it about—or that the burden of growing up is now transposed from me to my spouse." All these are dangerously false assumptions based on a mechanical rather than a centered view of man and life.

Third, if you already are married, but feel you should have waited, do not be precipitous. Do not rush out of one marriage or into another. Rather keep in mind that inner growth comes first and that the environment you have chosen is but an expression of your inner states (theme A3 of the master table—responsibility). Young married couples must be patient with their frustrations and disappointments. They must resolve to grow in their marriage. They must conclude that their decision to marry was not based on compatibility but on the decision to learn to grow together—with pains and joys.

Fourth, a society that expects and encourages two marriages of its people is likely to be a healthier one than the one we have at present. The first marriage is experimental; it is a learning experience, and a matter of sexual convenience. The second marriage—which may or may not be with the same partner—is permanent and can involve children.

Fifth, people in the middle of life must appreciate and recognize their fortunate position. They must take advantage of the possibilities for authentic love rather than discard them.

Sixth, and finally, society must separate once and for all love and sex, as well as marriage and children. Love can wait, sex cannot. Love and sex are not the same, and the need to equate them creates confusion and neuroses. Love is precious, not sex. Love is sacred, not sex. Love is holy, not sex. Sex *can* be holy, but it can also be cheap, with no loss to anyone. Love, on the other hand, exists only as a holy and sacred phenomenon. Sex is physical, love is a conscious or spiritual reality. Bad love does not exist. Bad love is no love at all. Love means divine, romantic, aesthetic love. With the advent of easily available contraceptives and legal abortions, the separation between love and sex is now, perhaps for the first time in the history of mankind, final. A new age of freedom for self-definition is upon us.

No cynicism whatever is intended in this analysis of the separation of love and sex, since it is of course possible and supremely desirable to make sex an expression of love. We will get to that point in later chapters.

EXISTENTIAL LOVE IS PREEROTIC OR AN-EROTIC

The *second* theme of existential love is that it is presexual, preerotic, prebiological, presomatic. It occurs essentially only on the level of pure consciousness; it is a transaction between one pure inward consciousness and another. The physical accoutrements are incidental, later, separate.

Existential love is not limited to a relation between different sexes. It can also exist between male and male, female and female, young and young, old and old, young and old, and between two or among many. It is the unique encounter of one consciousness with one other or many others that characterizes existential love. The physical aspects of the re-

lationship are a matter of subsequent choice. These physical manifesta-
tions are the result of decisions as to whether, when, and how to express
the love and are not necessary and integral components of the love
itself.

Existential love exists on the level of pure consciousness; and on that
level social distinctions and biological differences do not yet exist.
Existential love is an encounter of awarenesses; it is a spiritual encounter
of egos, a co-presence that has not yet translated itself into specific acts—
such as sexual intercourse or friendship—nor has existential love transformed itself into established social institutions—such as marriage and
children in a family. Existential love is thus closer to deep friendship
than to sexual relations.

MIRRORING

The *third* theme of existential love is the act of mirroring or reflecting.
The essence of man is his inner consciousness, his subjective center. This
center cannot be seen, measured, weighed, or objectified. *To be loved*
is to discover that center *in oneself through another*. *To love* is to discover this center *in another through oneself*.

The act of love is the phenomenon of encounter: It is the unique
mystery in which one conscious center witnesses another conscious center;
it is a copresence in which one existing ego confirms and validates the
reality of a second existing ego. The holy act of mirroring or of co-
perception is a two-pronged fork. In mirroring I for the first time experience and understand the uniqueness of my true conscious inwardness. It is the reflections in the other, the mirror effect of the other, the
response in depth of the other, the fact that the other is not a projection
of me but an impenetrable reality of its own, it is the recognition of me
by the other that makes clear to me *that* I am and *who* I am. This experience of the interpenetration of two independent freedoms is the integration of loving and being loved in the complex experience of existential love.

Let me explain this irreducible point, this untranslatable experience,
through metaphors. In empty space, even the most powerful light source,
from a klieg light to the sun itself, is, as it were, invisible to itself unless
it is reflected. The light of the sun is invisible on the sun unless and
until it is reflected by particles and bodies in the darkness of outer space.
A dust particle reflects a minuscule part of the sun, whereas a planet
reflects a great deal more. But the sun will never, shall we say, see itself
in its full glory until a cosmic mirror is held up to it. The mirror opens
up a brand new world, a never-before experienced dimension of reality.
The blinding brightness of the mirrored sun is a shattering confrontation
with the real sun. It is as if a second sun had suddenly been thrust

before it. The sun needs the cosmic mirror to perceive the glory and the uniqueness of what it means to be a sun. So it is with man: He needs a mirror to discover himself. And what can serve as mirror to his inward consciousness? Only another consciousness.

Let us consider a real mirror. Imagine that you were born on a deserted island and that you are as alone as Robinson Crusoe. You consequently have no way of knowing what you look like. You have felt your face many times—your nose, your mouth, your eyes, your cheeks, and chin—but you have never seen your face or anything even remotely like it. You suddenly come across a large mirror. For the first time, you see your face: You observe your eyes watching their own reflection in the mirror. You now know yourself—in a manner of speaking, you have been witnessed, validated, and in a true sense, become yourself. You now know who you are. You are now aware of what you look like. Whereas mercury- or silver-coated glass can reflect a face, only another inward subjective consciousness can reflect your own inwardness.

Consider the metaphor of travel. You are as a matter of actual fact born into a specific family, subculture, and country. As long as you do not travel you will take your demography and geography for granted and will not be aware of the fact that your social nature could be different. However, once you travel you see your family and your country, your personal habits and behavior patterns, through new and different eyes. In fact, from abroad you see your home for the first time as it truthfully is. Other cultures serve as mirror to your own tradition, which now—through mirroring—you see, understand, and appreciate for the first time. Mirroring means first that you discover yourself. It means that you feel loved—because you are loved.

The second prong of the fork of encounter is that you see—truly perceive, experience, and become aware of—a non-natural phenomenon. You see, in the mirroring aspect of love, another consciousness, a new subject, a different and independent inwardness. You now love another human being. That act of seeing is unlike any other kind of seeing. And so is that being which you see unlike any other event in the universe. Act and object are both unique, *sui generis*, and therefore inexplicable: These phenomena can only be experienced, they cannot be thought, conceptualized, or visualized.

To perceive the reality of another is also to give reality to that other. You now serve the function of mirroring to him. You bring about, to him and for him, his own reality. You thereby elicit his own nature and warrant his infinite respect and gratitude. You, as the sun, have discovered an actual new sun in the distance of space. You, as Robinson Crusoe, have discovered your real twin on the island.

In summary, the mirroring aspect of love is the act of mutual creation. It is self-creation and other-creation. *I am not* without the other and *the other is not* without me. But "other" and "me" are centers of consciousness, never bodies, personalities, or behavior systems. This point must never be forgotten.

RESISTANCE

In love, two consciousnesses are independent, not equatable, not interchangeable, not one, not continuous with each other. This is the *fourth* theme. The beloved will always be a person in his or her own right. Your beloved is never a mere extension of yourself. Also, your beloved is always different from you, and his or her existence will always and automatically affirm itself as different from yours. The mature adult, that is, the authentic individual, tolerates and welcomes the solid independence of the other consciousness. He can accept it; it gives him strength. However, the weak and immature, those who are not ready for love, will collapse under the weight of the independence of their beloved.

There is a crucial insight to be considered at this point: *The independence of the other consciousness permanently assures me that I am not alone in this world!* The independence of the other is the final cure for loneliness. Note the reversal: Many people feel lonely because the beloved is independent. But only the independent reality of the other can overcome the loneliness of the ego. A body can be an illusion; another person can be a dream. A kiss can be a fantasy. But a second witnessing and mirroring consciousness is always real and is always different from you. You can say to yourself, "I am never alone." The great philosophical problem of the existence of other minds—which has occupied the whole history of Western philosophy since Plato—is solved in the resistance experience of love.

Love that demands obedience or even slavery, love that uses rather than meets, is neurotic and lonely. But love that recognizes the ultimate reality of the other person is never lonely and is always healthy.

The following excerpt from a letter indicates the beautiful nature of independence and otherness. Some might be offended at the arrogance. I, on the other hand, responded warmly to the affirmation of independence, integrity, and resistance that it expresses. The letter tells me there exists another human being in this world, a being that in no manner of speaking is an extension of myself. The writer is one of my former students, deeply devoted to existentialism and its therapeutic uses.

Now that summer is fading and nearly three months have passed since you paid me the generous compliment of telling me that I deserve to receive a Ph.D., I have some serious thoughts on the matter which I feel will be of interest to you.

You made the observation that I am inflexible—true—I am also a committed existentialist—Sartrean persuasion. The idea of playing the graduate school game called "reinforce the professor's ego" appears to me to be symbolic suicide.

I am free, an individual, and respect my self-chosen constitution. I am devoted to scholarship—the investigation of "truth." I am not committed to the sad exercise of being careful not to offend a psychology professor's weak ego. If a psychology professor requires ego reinforcement from me, then he has nothing to offer me—he is a failure at his own profession. A graduate school must accept me for the student of existence that I am; there can be no compromise.

You I respect because you respect disagreement and place it in its proper perspective. From you one can learn.

But alas I must follow good Nietzsche's advice and honor you as my teacher by saying goodby to you as my teacher though not as my friend. My growth as a human being would be hindered if I were to always seek refuge in your camp. Please honor me by saying goodby to me as your student though not as your friend.

Sincerely,
Matthew C.

The letter and envelope bore no date and no return address.

WORSHIP

In love, the inward or transcendental ego discovers that its nature is to worship, which is the *fifth* theme. The being of consciousness is to reach out beyond itself. The most descriptive expression of that necessary outward reach is worship. Similarly, the sole reality that is worthy of worship is another transcendental inward center or consciousness. To recognize another inwardness is to have seen the sacred. Worship is the natural outgoing activity of the ego that has discovered its own essence. Worship is also the natural awed response to our perception of another consciousness. The common ground covered by love, sex, and religion becomes obvious in the phenomenon of worship. The nature of man is to reach beyond himself. That means he needs to be compassionate and to give. In *The Meaning of Service* Harry Emerson Fosdick wrote:

> *The Sea of Galilee and the Dead Sea are made of the same water. It flows down, clear and cool, from the heights of Hermon and the roots of the cedars of Lebanon. The Sea of Galilee makes beauty of it, for the Sea of Galilee has an outlet. It gets to give. It gathers in itself riches that it may pour them out again to fertilize the Jordan plain. But the Dead Sea with the same water makes horror. For the Dead Sea has no outlet. It gets to keep.*

The ultimate in the outward-reaching act of giving, in the flow of life from my center to the world beyond, is the expression of worship. To say "I worship you" is to reach out to you without thought of myself. Yet it is I who reach out. The capacity for worship must be nurtured if one is to be worthy of love.

3

Existential Love

The Therapeutic Model

Another aspect of authentic love is its therapeutic character, and that is the *sixth* theme.

MRS. McCABE'S THERAPY

A woman whom we shall call Mrs. McCabe was an unusually attractive person, in her late thirties, mother of two, married to an adequately successful dentist. She lived in Vancouver, British Columbia. Her marriage, although outwardly quite happy, was unfulfilling sexually and emotionally. She found no meaning in her marriage. She went through various types of therapy and finally established a meaningful relationship with a therapist whom we shall call Dr. Billings. Dr. Billings gave her intensive psychotherapy, focused mainly on encouraging Mrs. McCabe to get close to her feelings, especially her previously absent sense of femininity. Much progress was apparent. Mrs. McCabe identified increasingly with her femininity, with her role and sense of womanhood, something that had been conspicuously lacking in her pretherapeutic life. She began to look healthier and more feminine, to act more feminine, and dress more suggestively than she had before therapy. Mrs. McCabe was also now happier than before. Her values changed and she was open to life and love. She felt free, liberated.

The strong emphasis on the importance of femininity in therapy led to nudity, petting, and finally sexual intercourse between Mrs. McCabe and Dr. Billings. The goals of the therapy had been achieved; Mrs. Mc-Cabe was transformed from a frigid and rather abstract person into a sexualized and feminine woman; she was transformed from a woman with a dry and jejune lifestyle to a female with energy, strength, *joie de vivre,* and infinite capacity for all the good emotional potential life had to offer. There was no doubt that the rather extreme therapeutic measures used were effective, their possibly asocial and unprofessional character to the contrary notwithstanding.

But a shadow hung over the therapy. The therapy could not be terminated. It had gone on for over three years, was moving into its fourth, and even though everything appeared to have been resolved, both Dr. Billings and Mrs. McCabe felt that something important was missing. They did not know what. She had accomplished all she set out to achieve, but the therapy did not seem concluded. However, there was no further place to go.

The difficulty was cleared considerably by seeing it in the perspective of existential love. Dr. Billings came to realize the difference between an empirical and a transcendental relationship. After several consultations it became apparent that notwithstanding all precautions his relationship with Mrs. McCabe had become, in many respects, real rather than therapeutic, even though he did not think this was the case. He thought of himself as an existential therapist and felt that this meant he must get himself personally involved with his patients. He had forgotten the orthodoxy of distance, an orthodoxy taught not only by the psychoanalytic school but also by the existential-phenomenological approach to psychotherapy. He and Mrs. McCabe were at least partially in love with each other (empirical relationship) rather than in therapy (the transcendental relationship). A personal relation can never effect a permanent cure, since "cure" means independence of therapist and termination of therapy. Only when the therapist fades into the empty distance of the patient's consciousness can the therapy be said to be concluded. The resolution of a personal-involvement kind of therapy could only have come through a divorce for each and a new marriage to each other. But a therapist cannot marry each of his patients.

The solution adopted by Mrs. McCabe and Dr. Billings was to fully and openly *discuss* their deep physical and emotional relationship rather than *express* it, to discuss and analyze their need for each other rather than to live it. The sole justification for expressing feelings of affection in therapy is to produce material for subsequent therapeutic analysis and use. The feelings had merit in themselves, especially since Mrs. McCabe was not aware of them before. It was important for her to discover her great capacity for orgasms and her delight in being coquettish. But that was not enough. She had to reflect on these emotions, understand what they meant and integrate them into a whole life. In so doing, she is now relating herself on a level of greater freedom and control, with the promise of ultimate human fulfillment.

Mrs. McCabe and Dr. Billings are now *reflecting on* their feelings rather than being their feelings.

Because of their intimate emotional and physical involvement, Mrs. McCabe and Dr. Billings found they had extremely valuable material for therapeutic distancing and mutual discussion. They could discuss non-erotically their mutual intercourse and talk nonromantically about their deeply felt love for each other. In so doing, they completely redefined their relationship. Their connection and their love were now moved to a transcendental level, to the region of pure consciousness and pure inwardness. Their relationship was now closer than ever before, but it was transcendental rather than empirical. It was now therapeutic rather than personal, universal rather than exclusive. It was a true meeting and no longer a using. By living principle C 3 of the master table, both were now free.

The result of the distancing was that therapy could be successfully terminated. Both had gained their independence. Mrs. McCabe developed the strength to be self-reliant and to exist emotionally on her own, because that is the meaning of the secure realm of pure consciousness. She found her true home—the strength of her pure consciousness rather than the arms of her therapist. The same was true of Dr. Billings. The therapeutic relationship had been elevated to the region of pure transcendental consciousness and at that moment separation and independence became obvious, easy, and natural.

A Transcendental Relationship

A therapeutic relationship, like existential love, is "transcendental." It is a relationship that exists on the level of pure consciousness and not on the level of empirical, objective, and worldly reality alone. It is a mind-to-mind encounter and not solely a feeling or emotional experience. A transcendental relationship is one consciousness discovering another consciousness and not one body judging another body. It recognizes the reality of the other but does not necessarily involve deep feelings of attachment or revulsion for the other. It goes beyond the mutual exchange of feelings. Because of these features an orthodox therapeutic relationship can serve as a model for an authentic existential encounter or authentic existential love.

An orthodox therapeutic relationship is a relationship of mutual discovery, care, and concern. It is a relationship of ultimate respect. If the patient "loves" the therapist, that is not real love; it is instead called a "transference neurosis." The effect of this kind of labeling is to distance the patient from his feelings of love. He perceives his love now as an object that must be therapeutically investigated rather than an emotion that must be lived. That distance from an emotion is a key to understanding existential love.

It is of course possible for patient and therapist to love each other or to hate each other. That occurs in what in phenomenology we call the empirical or psychological realm. It is a relation of one empirical ego to another. If their love is empirical, it may end in marriage, as it did in F. Scott Fitzgerald's *Tender Is the Night*. But patient and therapist could also, instead, and after the feelings have been expressed, talk about the feeling of love (or hate) that may exist between them. If they marry, their relationship is empirical, which means it is nontherapeutic or antitherapeutic. If they discuss the deeper meanings of these feelings, and if there is a fee and a time restriction that rigorously define the outer limits of the relationships, then their encounter is transcendental—it goes beyond the felt emotions involved.

It is important to have a clear idea of the difference between being romantically in love and talking professionally about a particular feeling that is present between patient and therapist. In the latter case, the feeling is like any object that rests at a distance before them in the consulting room, which is visible to both patient and therapist. As they talk about that feeling, a new, nonfeeling relationship develops between the two. And that new type of distant and somewhat ethereal and rational closeness is the paradigm for a therapeutic relationship. Point C 3, reflection, on the master table ("I am able to both *live* my life and to *reflect* on my life"), establishes the basis for such a meeting of two conscious freedoms.

This transcendental closeness is more intimate than if it were sexual; it is also nonexclusive and nonenvious and therefore does not lead to jealousy or competitiveness. Transcendental love—which is existential love—when based on the therapeutic model offers no threat to anyone. The existential love of a married woman and her therapist is no threat to her husband nor to the therapist's wife.

Transcendental love is open to all people. All marriages between nonschizophrenics can, in principle, be transformed from empirical or purely psychological relationships into spiritual or transcendental encounters. All good marriages can be improved, all mediocre marriages can be made successful and deepened, and all those marriages which define themselves as failures can be saved and then transformed into healthy relationships with meaningful encounters. What is required is the establishment of a transcendental relationship. That is the top priority.

Let me summarize. Patient and therapist are two transcendental freedoms. Before them lies *one* object: The patient's feelings (in the case of transference) or the feelings of both patient and therapist (in the case of a countertransference). They relate to each other not by being or by expressing these feelings but by openly discussing and shrewdly observing these feelings. The feelings exist at a distance from *both* inward egos. Both living egos become pure transcendental consciousnesses in the therapeutic hour. They join as pure conscious egos, as transcendental egos, and thus have the deepest of all possible human relationships: existential love.

A therapeutic relationship is open, accepting and tolerant. Years ago, Carl Rogers aptly described it as an atmosphere of "unqualified positive regard." That description is still one of the clearest and finest evocations of a transcendental encounter.

Many modern schools of therapy disagree with this ideal of detachment. To them, therapy means personal involvement, culminating sometimes even in sexual intercourse. Unfortunately, some of these schools espousing deep and real relations between therapist and patient call themselves existential. In truth, the existential approach is to be measured by mental attitude, not behavior. Therapy as a model for existential love is rather distant and intellectual. If the two individuals do become physically and emotionally involved, therapeutic use must be made of the relationship, and therapeutic interpretations must take precedence over personal feelings. The key concept lies in the word "distance."

If there should ever be any emotional or physical relation between patient and therapist, even a handshake or a hug, it must be used therapeutically. If the physical or emotional relationship is accepted at face value, then the relationship has ceased to be therapeutic (i.e., transcendental) and has become personal or real (i.e., empirical). At that moment the therapy is over and real life has taken its place. However, if the relationship between patient and therapist is perceived from a distance (what in existentialism is called an "epoche" or a "phenomenological reduction") then it is authentic, therapeutic. That distance, disengagement, and disinvolvement is achieved in orthodox psychotherapy by referring to the relationship as *neurotic*. Such terms are successful techniques and facilitating devices for creating distance; their effect is to remove the relationship from the empirical level of social relations and elevate it to the level of love or to that of a transcendental relationship. In other words, calling patient-therapist love a transference neurosis is an act of authentic existential love.

REMEMBER

1. If you desire love, do not look for boys and girls or men and women but work on your own inner growth.
2. Love is for adults only.

3. Love is the ability to give up the pleasures and the possessions of this world.

4. For most people, romantic love is ahead of them rather than already past.

5. Do not be in a hurry to marry or to change your marital status if you are already married.

6. Marriage does not mean happiness but rather the opportunity to grow up together.

7. Plan on two marriages—hopefully but not necessarily to the same person.

8. Love is not the same as sex.

9. Love can exist without sex, marriage, and the family.

10. Love is mutual respect and recognition.

11. Love is the discovery of your own spiritual center by means of your discovery of the spiritual center of another person. This is the meaning of *being loved.*

12. Love is your own personal perception of the spiritual center of another person. This is the meaning of *loving.*

13. Love is the creation of oneself and the creation of another.

14. The only thing in this world that can serve as a mirror to your consciousness is the willing consciousness of another human being.

15. Your consciousness, and only your consciousness can serve as a mirror to another consciousness.

16. In true love, you accept fully the independence of your lover.

17. Love is honesty.

18. If your lover disappoints or contradicts you, remember that he (or she) is proving to you that you are not alone in this world.

19. Love is to request the opposition or resistance of the beloved.

20. Love is the desire for worship.

21. If you wish to love you must be able to worship.

22. Love is also like a therapeutic relationship: it is distance, closeness, and responsibility all in one.

23. There is an important difference between a consciousness-to-consciousness relationship (transcendental) and a body-to-body or role-to-role relationship (empirical). Only the former is existential love.

24. Only through distance can you achieve intimacy.

4

Existential Love

Surrender and Care

The elements of ideal love discussed in the previous chapter are only part of the total picture. Existential and authentic love embraces many more important characteristics. We now turn to these.

SURRENDER-CONQUEST

The voluntary surrender of one freedom to another is central to the experience of love. This is the *seventh* theme of existential love. The surrender is never forced. The one who surrenders demands to be received as one who surrenders, not as one who is defeated. Only a true freedom can surrender voluntarily.

The converse of the experience of surrender is the experience of appropriation, ownership, or conquest; that is also part of the definition of existential love.

The cliché is that man conquers and possesses while woman surrenders and submits; the man *wants* to conquer and the woman *wants* to surrender. But the male-female relationship can be reversed with impunity. Existential love is presexual, prebiological, presomatic. Only a separate decision to express existential love (a transcendental phenomenon) through two bodies, and through social institutions, renders the accidental biological and social features with which we are born meaningful and relevant.

Thus, the center of surrender can reside without difficulty in the male and that of conquest in the female. Or, of course, such a relationship

28

can even exist between members of the same sex, as in the case of teacher and student, especially if the teacher is perceived by the student as a great master—as Czerny perceived his teacher Beethoven, or as a religious aspirant experiences his Zen master or his guru.

Through surrender and conquest two independent transcendental freedoms, two inwardnesses, can come closest to one another. This union is a mystery because it is the experience of being two and one at the same time, like a magnet, where positive and negative poles are different but nevertheless form the essential and inseparable ingredients of *one* magnetic field.

The mysterious sense of unity in love, the oneness of two atomic and irreducible entities is never forced; it is always voluntary. But it is also total: The voluntary and free surrender, like the conquest, is so total that it is embarrassing. These are "embarrassing" phenomena because they are completely different from and contrary to ordinary, everyday transactions. Therefore, love is done in secret and accompanied with shame. Love, or better, transcendental love, to be perceived as the deep experience that it is, must be felt from the inside out. It is an experience that must be seen *from* the windows of our inwardness *out to* the world of the other. Then it is not shameful. However, if we perceive love from the outside in, from the point of view of an external observer, then love is a bizarre animal act or a psychotic act, because we perceive only its adventitious, empirical nature and totally overlook its essential transcendental nature.

THE SURRENDER OF FREEDOM

The lover who conquers holds something that is entirely too big to hold. He holds in his hands a radioactive sun—a human freedom. He holds that freedom not because he has conquered it, not because he has acquired it by his own powers or merits, but because it is freely given to him through an act of grace, through an offering of pure generosity. That makes the conquest of the surrending love completely undeserved. The true conquering lover says "I want you to be mine," but immediately he wisely adds, "I do not deserve you."

Similarly, the freedom that surrenders gives not just himself, but gives *all there is.* Surrender in love is an act without reservations. The joy in surrender is in the act itself—the act of total abandonment, total faith, total self-loss.

Before self-loss is safe, a trustworthy other or partner must be found. And who is trustworthy? It is the person willing to possess such total surrender. The conqueror is never perfect in real life. Love, therefore, depends richly on the imagination and on illusion. But a beautiful illusion it is! If the lovers know that they are living an illusion, then their love is authentic. Then they have both honest realism and romantic ecstasy. Their love is inauthentic only when they confuse the mystic bliss of a loving encounter with the hard facts of social and psychological reality.

Rarely has the intensity of the unity of two, the inseparableness of two independent freedoms in love, been more expressively stated than in these lines from Edgar Allan Poe:

> And neither the angels in Heaven above
> Nor the demons down under the sea,
> Can ever dissever my soul from the soul
> Of the beautiful Annabel Lee.

It is difficult for surrender and conquest to be the basis for a realistic human relationship or for useful social institutions. The Roman ideal of the *paterfamilias* and the old-fashioned Moslem marriage are examples of making real and permanent the surrender-conquest relationship. In the ecstatic moment of love, surrender and conquest have deep meaning. But as a total lifestyle, as a permanent institution, such a relationship damages all other aspects of life. This is the case in our society. Among self-aware men and women, however, surrender and possession remain as eternal features of existential love.

ILLUSION AND REALITY

Every mature human being must integrate the contradiction between reality and illusion into his life. The authentic individual can be both an idealist and a realist, as circumstances warrant, realizing that whichever his choice may be some values are destroyed. The idealist destroys the practical; the realist destroys the spirit. But that ambiguity is the essence of human life. To be human means to be a contradiction. This point is made in theme C 14 of the master table ("the inescapable ambiguities and contradictions of life are my powerful allies"). The authentic individual has made the confrontation with ambiguity a central project in his life. In fact, he has absorbed ambiguity into his being. He recognizes that the essence of his humanity, because he is an ego-to-world consciousness, is to be an ambiguous field. To deplore ambiguity is to become his own enemy.

In democratic society, the surrender-conquest syndrome can be neither legislated nor institutionalized. It can exist ethically only if it is chosen freely by the couple that has decided to create love.

Love, then, involves not only ego-gratification and centeredness but also its opposite, surrender. Many people resist this truth. But that resistance is itself a strong index of inauthenticity. Such responses as "That's impractical." "It's too idealistic," "I like my independence and I surrender to no one" are the exclamation of people afraid to meet, afraid to love fully. It is an agonizing sight and a frustrating experience to approach a handsome or beautiful person, whose body invites love, only to discover the icy coldness and insular distance of that beautiful person.

The surrender-conquest syndrome, central to the phenomenon of love, is possible only once. It is from this fact that we derive the importance of first love. Surrender is at its most authentic when its possibility was not even considered.

As a substitute for lost first love, some individuals repeatedly choose new partners.

CARE, COMMITMENT, DUTY, AND DEVOTION

The *eighth* fundamental aspect of existential love is the decision to *care* for the other consciousness. Parent-child relationships, especially around the time of birth, are the models here.

In existential love it is not enough to be a witness or a mirror. The separate decision to make a commitment—a dedication, a choice of duty —to that other consciousness is an essential ingredient of love. An animal cannot make a commitment: Only a free human being can make the decision to care.

It is important for the reader who wants to understand his relation to love to ask himself the following questions: "Am I the kind of person who can make a commitment to another human being? Am I a responsible human being? Can I be devoted and loyal? Self-sacrificing? Generous? Kind and compassionate?" Look at your past life and your present human relationships, and answer honestly.

Many people are quite unable to make commitments to others. "Have you decided that there is another human being in your life who is more important than you are?" "Is there a person in this world for whom you are irreplaceable?" "What does your relation to that person disclose about you?" "If you had to sacrifice an organ—such as a kidney—or even your very own life, could you do it?" "Can you make such a deep commitment to another person?" In authentic love you care for your child, for example, but that does not imply that you demand reciprocation. How do you stand in this aspect of life? There is no room for buying and bartering in love. There are no contracts, treaties, or negotiations in love.

In existential love, the commitment is unqualified. It says "I care for you because I have chosen to care for you. I demand nothing in return. I expect nothing. My decision to care has no strings attached. I do not care so as to achieve ulterior purposes. I care solely because I choose to care." The decision to care is self-sacrificing. For consciousness to move out into the world as the decision to care is a privilege. "The pleasure of love is in loving," wrote La Rochefoucauld, "We are happier in the passion we feel than in what we arouse." Similarly, Lamartine wrote, "To love for the sake of being loved is human, but to love for the sake of loving is angelic."

The often-maligned promise to love in the marriage ceremony makes authentic sense. *This is a decision to care.* We cannot promise to feel specific emotions in the future. But only a thoroughly biological, materialistic orientation to love (one based on the ghost-in-the-machine theory of man) will equate love exclusively with feeling. An existential conception (based on the field-of-consciousness theory of man) recognizes that love includes the element of choice, of decision. Love is a function of both the transcendental and the empirical, the subjective and the objective poles of the field of consciousness. Therefore, a promise to love in the marriage ceremony is fully justified.

Specifically, the decision to care is the chosen devotion to the demands and needs of another consciousness or of the empirical ego that surrounds that consciousness. Thus, a mother chooses to care for her child —as a subjective personality and in addition as a bundle of objective biological and psychological needs that surround the transcendental conscious center that is this child. A husband chooses to care for his wife. The proof of the authenticity of either decision is poignantly discovered if the child or wife becomes an invalid.

Preston

Preston's wife—with whom he had an excellent twenty-six-year marriage—became an invalid after a massive stroke at age fifty-three, on a camping trip near the Grand Canyon. They returned to Los Angeles, and Preston chose to care for her without apparent reward and at the cost of much loss and denial in his own life. Nevertheless, he welcomed the opportunity fate had offered him to choose care, to decide for authentic love. His wife's transcendental center was intact, but her stroke made that silent center almost inaccessible to her external surrounding world. Preston chose to meet her physical needs and thus to offer a sacrifice of care to her almost permanently hidden center. For him, that was a privileged opportunity. At first Preston resented the changes required in his life by his wife's invalidism. He had to put up with her constant depression, her anger, her irascibility, and her ingratitude. In addition, Preston was forced to spend money he did not have on medicine, special treatments, and equipment. He purchased a van and had it specially modified to accommodate her wheelchair. He took her to visit friends and parks, attend concerts and movies, and encouraged her to travel. She never really thanked him, but her body told him that he was doing the right thing to the transcendental consciousness hiding inside. Because of

Preston's decision to care unilaterally, that is, without reward, his wife's silent consciousness was far more peaceful than it would have otherwise remained. He learned that to give without receiving, that to reach out to another consciousness without expectation of return—in the sure knowledge that one's love is absolutely needed—is one of the great possibilities of human existence.

As a result of his decision for authentic love, Preston found new time and energy for himself. After he made the decision to cope, he developed new interests and friends. He had been mechanically inclined, excellent with pliers and solder, with wires and transistors, tubes and speakers. Now he branched out into literature and philosophy, art and music. He had been an asocial individual; now he cultivated new friends and associations. And Preston made the rewarding discovery that his newly expanded life did not conflict with his wife's invalidism. In fact, she responded well to his increased freedom. Heretofore, Preston had felt sorry for himself and restricted himself to his house, just as his wife was restricted to her room. His loving dedication and commitment to her true center—rather than resentment of her paralyzed body—introduced expanded space and time into *both* their lives. It seems hard to believe, but his wife's stroke actually rejuvenated Preston's previously sterile life. No ordinary success, like a million-dollar windfall in the New York State lottery, would have achieved as much.

Willard

In Dallas, Willard was stricken with an incurable lung cancer at age forty-nine, after twenty years of a good and active marriage. He rapidly lost weight and looked emaciated. His wife, Velma, made the decision to care for him to the end. At first, Willard was intractable and irascible; he threw tantrums like an infant, both in the hospital and at home. Velma chose not to respond to his yelling and flailing body but to the serene pure consciousness behind it all, a consciousness that was at the time inaccessible even to Willard himself, but a consciousness that wanted to be heard. We must not forget that the center is silent. But what is silence? Adelaide Crapsey (1878–1914) evoked it magnificently when she wrote (in *Cinquain Triad*):

> These be
> Three silent things:
> The falling snow . . . the hour
> Before the dawn . . . the mouth of one
> Just dead.

Velma's devotion was a sign to Willard that his disease, like his death, could be accepted. Through her adult behavior, Velma signaled to Willard's center that she had chosen to cope. Such a choice is always elevating and inspiring to those privileged to witness it. It was to Willard, who also chose to cope rather than to "cop out." As a result of Velma's self-sacrificing and unilateral love, Willard improved enough to become a volunteer professional cancer counselor, helping others cope with what he too had to cope. He found his meaning in his despair—which is an idea found in principles C 1 and C 2 of the master table ("I choose to value my pains" and "I choose to value my limitations"). His new role was to visit patients matched to him in age, personality, occupation, and cancer-type. He helped others die with dignity and aplomb, and he did the same for himself. His inner strength—in the most desperate of all situations—was a gift given to him, with no desire for reward, by the commitment to care made by Velma at the onset of his fatal illness. He died two years later, although experts had given him only six months to live.

5
Existential Love
Natural and Ineffable

Love Is Natural

It is natural to love and it is natural for love to be spiritual first and physical second. This is the *ninth* theme of existential love. It is natural for love to begin as my full awareness of *my* conscious center and my full awareness of *your* conscious center. Only then is it natural for love to be translated into the feelings and expressions of my body, your body, marriage, family, and children. Love is a pure stream that has its subjective source in high snow-capped mountains amidst clear blue skies—the realm of pure consciousness—and then winds its way, like Smetana's *Moldau,* through the fields and the forests—the body and its personality—until it finally and with growing vigor reaches the majestic sea—the reality of the world, rich with other people and natural beauties, a world that resists our desires but can also fulfill them.

Dominated as we are today by the ghost-in-the-machine theory of man, especially in the behavioral sciences such as psychology and sociology, the conviction that consciousness is prior to the body and society is thought outlandish, and its exponents are anathematized. In view of this dangerously entrenched materialistic misconception of humanity, the existential view, the field-of-consciousness theory, must be taken especially seriously, though without reverting to medieval or Victorian disembodied self-denial and unfeeling distortion of our natural love for the body, the sensuous, and the physical.

Why is love natural? "Natural" means to be in harmony with our nature as human beings. And our nature is expressed in the field-of-consciousness theory. Thus, the nature of consciousness is to reach out into the world. We call that reaching out or emerging "growth"—the experience of ourselves as "time." That endless reaching beyond our present situation is the self-transcending character of consciousness. And consciousness moves from its inward center, through the body and out into the world of society, nature, and other inwardnesses or conscious centers. Related to this concept are themes C 12 and C 13 of the master table ("I experience time as living in a present which, while utilizing the past, connects directly and primarily into my future," and "My life is an endless process of growing, emerging, and reaching out").

Like a river which exists only as long as it flows, human existence is real and vital only as long as it transcends itself, as long as it grows beyond itself.

No word better describes this process of self-transcendence than "love." For consciousness to *reach out* is for the center to *give;* consciousness meets the challenge of the "other" when the center encounters and witnesses in love.

Not all that exists under the name of love is natural. Love that starts with the body or with society is learned—that love is a game, with rules that can be changed and relearned. Authentic love moves from inside to outside, as an expression of inwardness. Love that begins with the teachings of society is distorted by a ghost-in-the-machine theory of man. Love that starts with physical erotic stimulation is thus "unnatural" love. A Los Angeles woman, recently mentioned in the news, is serving time in jail because in her nightclub, as a special attraction, she performed "the act of love" on stage each night at midnight. Calling that act of sexual intercourse "the act of love" shows utter ignorance of the nature of love. It implies that love is a mechanical function like the winding of a watch, rather than consciousness flowing out into the world.

On the other hand, love that starts at the center, that is, that begins with consciousness and then is translated into the sensuous and social externality is fully natural, in harmony with the nature of man. Existential love reestablishes human relations as the center of our existence. This perhaps is the most basic proof of its naturalness. An inevitable consequence of this in the larger society must be indignation whenever a person uses rather than meets other people.

Society needs only one law: respect consciousness. Even such a relatively minor offense as inconsiderate driving—racing noisily down a street full of small children at play—is not to be tolerated. Disrespect for a human consciousness is never to be tolerated, be it a discourtesy or a nuclear war.

In sum, to love is to express the natural motion of human consciousness, whereas to truncate that self-transcendence through a materialistic disregard of what is human in persons is to violate nature.

That love is the natural motion of being is expressed in the words of the poet Shelley:

> All love is sweet,
> Given or returned,
> *Common as light is love,*
> And its familiar voice wearies not ever. . . .
> (Italics mine)

LOVE IS INEFFABLE

The *tenth* and last theme of existential love is that the encounter of two conscious freedoms is an experience that is unique, *sui generis,* and ineffable. It is an irreducible experience that must be had to be understood. Edgar Allan Poe showed an understanding of the ineffability of love when he wrote:

> And this maiden she lived with no other thought,
> Than to love and be loved by me.
> *She* was a child and *I* was a child,
> In this kingdom by the sea,
> But we loved with a love that was more than love—
> I and my Annabel Lee—
> With a love that the wingéd seraphs of Heaven
> Coveted her and me.

We cannot express in literal words the nature of existential love because words refer to the world and not to the consciousness that observes the world. And existential love is a transcendental phenomenon, a relation between pure consciousnesses. No difficulty exists in experiencing existential love. Referring to it with scientific terms rather than through metaphor or poetry is another matter altogether. The ineffability of love means that continuing new experiences are open to those who look upon maturing as a beautiful and unending adventure.

RETURN TO RHODA, RUTH, AND STEPHANIE

In light of the above, let us take a brief second look at one of the three letters from the beginning of Chapter 1 and its ideal relation to sex.

Stephanie wants to conform to accepted social standards. That is her first mistake. For one, she is capable of love; she loves her husband and is willing to enhance and increase that love. In other words, there is much right with her and in her love. Above all, she is right, proper, and true in her own eyes and in her own scale of values. Furthermore, she thinks that if she manipulates her psyche—her behavior and her responses—to conform to meaningless and temporary standards, standards not based on the fundamental nature of man but on current fashions, then she will find happiness and love. Manipulation of body and behavior is the therapy of a ghost-in-the-machine theory of man. But Stephanie needs confirmation in her love, assurance that she is capable of love and, above all, that she is free to define her own expression of that love. She has made the fatal error of identifying a loving and meaningful life with a technically correct orgasm. A letter from a young woman describes that condition—that disastrous piece of misinformation —very well:

> *I have suddenly been forced to face a problem I'd managed to keep submerged for years, and I desperately need help in its solution. If you could possibly recommend avenues toward some counseling, I would be very grateful.*
>
> *At 22, I remain unable (unwilling?) to reach sexual climax. This hasn't previously been of particular importance, since during and after my marriage I have proved successful in concealing my lack of response from any sexual partners. However, I am now in love with a man so sensitive to me that he has discovered this lack. My reaction, through extreme anxiety, guilt, and shame, was tremendous hostility with complete refusal to admit, let alone discuss, the problem.*
>
> *I'm sure this problem will quickly destroy our relationship, the best and most fulfilling I've ever experienced, due to my feelings of shame. At this point I couldn't even consider a sexual encounter with a man who is aware of my inadequacy.*
>
> *I've tried following my anxieties, and it seems obvious that my fears involve a symbolic death—since I am an intellectual, independent person (considered masculine traits), an inability to respond sexually destroys my already weak view of myself as a woman. On the other hand, I have a suspicion that the reason I don't relax enough to achieve a climax has something to do with the feeling that I would be losing myself in complete surrender. My overall view of sex is a maze of contradiction, from intellectual acceptance of virtually anything to emotional distress when applied personally. . . .*
>
> *Sincerely,*

The center of man and woman is not the orgasm but the inward consciousness. The writer of the letter needs support in the rectitude of her self-disclosure, not better techniques for an improved orgasm-reflex. She needs to build the center, not replace her body with a new model.

Stephanie's interest in yoga is genuine. It is her way of being in touch with her center. She must learn to respect what her yoga is and what it means to her; and she must insist that those close to her respect it as well. Changing what she intuitively knows is right for her is wrong.

My first bit of advice to Stephanie is to give up the effort to change and to accept herself for what she is. I accept her that way and, probably, so does her husband and so do her children. It is now up to her to accept herself that way as well.

Options

My second recommendation is that she has four basic options. They reflect the way she chooses to connect her center to her world, how she chooses to be embodied:

1. She changes her center to fit her world. That is what she is trying to do now and probably has tried to do all her life—without success. The project which transforms or eradicates the center does not work. It leads to frustration and despair because it *eliminates or displaces the center;* it moves the center outward, into foreign territory. That solution demands that Stephanie change her philosophic nature—and this she cannot do. The center does the eradicating; it cannot eliminate itself. Also, if the center moves out, away from the center, it is the center at the center that does the moving—another contradiction!

2. She can dissociate herself from her husband, through death, psychosis, or separation, since she cannot live with the guilt of her sexual failure. That solution would work in part, except that her more superficial needs and her family values would go unfulfilled. This is an inauthentic solution and out of it new and different guilts would develop.

3. She can put up with the situation, do her "duty" and keep her center unaffected. She can build a wall and protectively, like an ascetic, isolate her center. To do her duty means to cook even though she hates it, as a person would do any unpleasant job that needs doing—such as cleaning toilets, washing dishes, and mopping the floor. Above all, to do her duty is to have sex with her husband when he requests it—even though she hates it! The secret for the success of this option lies in the *Bhagavad-Gita's* prescription for action that is detached from the fruits of the action: "The truly admirable man controls his senses by the power of his will. All his actions are disinterested." And later, "Do your duty, always; but without attachment. That is how a man reaches the ultimate truth by working without anxiety about results." *

If necessary, it is perfectly possible for any human being to live in his center and perform whatever worldly or dutiful acts are necessary or are chosen by him as desirable. This solution is neither as difficult or as painful as it seems. As a matter of fact, the solution for Stephanie was to accept the directions in which she was moving anyway as the right ones for her. She felt relief and peace when she discovered that her re-

* Swami Prabhavananda and Christopher Isherwood, trans., *Bhagavad-Gita* (London: Phoenix House, 1947), p. 52. Reprinted by permission of the Vedanta Society of Southern California and J M Dent & Sons Ltd.

treat into the center through the strength yoga could give her was a legitimate and healthy solution. What she had *not* known is that acts can be performed with detachment, out of a sense of self-imposed duty, and that such detachment is both healthy and moral.

This solution is certainly not the end of Stephanie's problem. However, having reached the security of her center, she is now in the position of power to choose whether to remain there or whether to become embodied, if she so desires; and if so, how she is to constitute or organize her embodiment.

4. There is of course a final option open to Stephanie. She can integrate the inner and the outer worlds in which she lives. She is at present ready for existential love but not for existential sex. (The authentic integration of consciousness with the sensuous and the bodily will be discussed in the next chapters.)

Rhoda

Rhoda's case is simpler. Rhoda wants love. Her problem is that she thinks love is sex. She has thus reversed the direction of the flow of human consciousness. For Rhoda consciousness moves from the world to her conscious center, from body to consciousness. (This is the reverse of its natural motion.) And Rhoda lives according to that belief. Since it is a false, a counterfactual belief, her life rebels through symptoms such as dissatisfaction and guilt. The answer for her is that love is prior to sex, love brings about sex, and love results from authenticity. Love for Rhoda does not depend on finding the "right guy."

Ruth

Finally, there is Ruth. First, one suspects that much more than meets the eye is going on in Ruth's mind. She demands a fundamental redefinition of the institution of marriage. That is legitimate. Her error lies in expecting her husband to go along with her in this reconstruction of an ancient social institution. That was not his understanding as he entered marriage. She cannot change the contract in the middle of life without dramatic consequences. She also seriously underestimates the difficulty most people face in redefining fundamental institutions. To redefine the marriage relation is not a conceptual or an intellectual matter alone; it is the concern of a person's total being. I doubt that Ruth has the inner strength and self-knowledge necessary to carry out the life-long project of redefining the relationship between the sexes. Ruth has the *right* ideas—in the sense that they conform to the criteria of the master table—but not yet the right self-disclosure.

REMEMBER

Ask yourself, "Is there love in my life?" Existential love—a prerequisite to existential sex—has been described in this and previous chapters as having the following fifteen characteristics. Remember them!

1. Love is capable of the free total surrender of one's life.
2. To be able to love is to be able to give up everything for the beloved.
3. To be worthy of love is to be worthy of receiving the total surrender of another freedom.
4. To love is to be realistic about the claim that an illusion has on mankind.
5. Love is the decision to care for another without expecting rewards.
6. The parent-child relationship is one of the great teachers of love.
7. To love is to appreciate the opportunity to make a commitment to another.
8. Love is to permanently reach beyond oneself.
9. Love is the experience of personal growth.
10. Love that starts with mechanical erotic stimulation is contrary to the philosophical nature of man.
11. Love teaches us that human relationships are the essence of life.
12. Love is an ineffable experience—experienceable but indescribable, because it is completely unique.
13. Love exists in an atmosphere of total acceptance.
14. Love is the ability to forgive your enemies.
15. Love is the experience of the unity of two freedoms.

TEST YOURSELF

It is not enough to have a theoretical understanding of existential love; these ideas must be integrated into life. Two approaches present themselves: measurement and exercise. To measure is to assess and evaluate the extent to which these ideas are actually put into practice by you. And exercise is the systematic effort to bring about increased integration.

For each of the themes on the following test ask yourself: "Is there evidence, based on my own past experience (not on my present intuition), that I am capable of entering into the kind of relationship described?" Rate yourself on a scale of seven, "1" means "totally incapable" and "7" means "fully competent." On this scale, "4" signifies neutrality or indecision.

Let us take an example. In number 3, a score of "1" indicates that you are totally incapable of perceiving either yourself or your partner as independent, as worthy of respect and recognition. In number 12, a

"7" answer means that you find it easy and welcome to share with a person who is nevertheless completely independent, even stubborn.

The test on the attached table is based on the fifteen characteristics of love outlined above. Take the test slowly and thoughtfully, and score yourself. A typical score is 70 out of a possible 105. Since the test is a subjective measure, its importance lies not in your absolute score but in your change of score over a period of time during which you expect growth to take place.

Now, using the same test, rate a person with whom you are in a close relationship.

Ask that person to rate himself (or herself) and then to rate you.

Compare results!

QUESTIONNAIRE ON EXISTENTIAL LOVE

(Take only after reading the previous four chapters—otherwise the concepts will be unfamiliar.)

Reflect on and react to the following statements on the basis of proven past experience and not on present intuitions. Use the following scale:

Scale	1	2	3	4	5	6	7
	Totally incapable			Neutral: Undecided about my ability			Fully competent

SCORE

1. I can give and accept love without expressing it in sex, marriage, and/or family. _____

2. I am capable of adult behavior most of the time. _____

3. I am able to fully respect and recognize the integrity of another human being. _____

4. I am able to experience an encounter in which I feel created into an individual and in which I know I am validating another freedom. _____

5. I can care, be devoted, and do my duty—without qualification—for another person of my choice. _____

6. I can create an atmosphere of openness and acceptance. _____

7. I can be honest with those I am close to. _____

8. I can fully surrender in the act of love. _____

9. I am able to worship another inward consciousness. _____

10. I can be ascetic and give up the pleasures and possessions of this world. _____

11. I am prepared to forgive my enemies. _____

12. I can tolerate the sometimes stubborn independence of those close to me. _____

13. I know that I am able to experience the inexplicable mysteries of love as the witness of two freedoms.   _____

14. I can grow emotionally, intellectually, and interpersonally without end.   _____

15. I can feel permanently identified with another human being.   _____

TOTAL SCORE   _____

ARE THERE LOVE EXERCISES?

In fact, there exist no exercises for love. Love is a far too serious business to permit of preparation or practice. Love is like conducting a great orchestra. There is no good way to practice the "instrument" which is the orchestra. The neophyte conductor cannot hire himself an orchestra on which to practice for hours and hours the way a violinist practices on his instrument.

Love is a risk that can be performed only by an authentic human being. An orchestra can be conducted only by one who has already earned the respect of its members and the public as an accomplished musician.

Love can be learned by example, experience, and exposure. Orchestra conducting, likewise, can be learned by long association with music and musicians and exposure to accomplished conductors.

Love is life and not a game. There are no games in which to practice love. In love, man is the self-transcending nature of his consciousness. He can only love; he cannot substitute for love.

6

From Sexual Prison to Sexual Paradise

Perversions and the Power of Freedom

Having explored the primary features of existential love, we should be ready to discuss the integration of that loving, intimate encounter with the sexual functions of our biological organism. Making love sexual, or biological, remains a choice, however—which we can fashion, creatively and artistically—and not an unavoidable obligation on our part. It follows that we can interpret the meaning of our sexual desires and organize our sexual potential along lines that are totally foreign to what I here call existential sex. Existential sex is the integration of the body with the structure of consciousness, following the outlines of the field-of-consciousness theory of man. But such integration is not required; this and the next chapter are devoted to what are usually termed sexual perversions or aberrations, for perversions are free choices regarding the uses of our sexuality, choices that do not conform to the field-of-consciousness personality theory outlined in the master table.

You are responsible for your sexual choices. If the latter are inauthentic, that is, if they do not conform to an awareness- and consciousness-centered view of man, but to a mechanical and materialistic ghost-in-the-machine theory, then you must hold yourself responsible for the organization of your world and you should be so held by others. You then have the power of your freedom to adjust and accept or change and re-create yourself. Similarly, if your sexual choices are authentic, then you can feel proud and strong because, again, you assume responsibility for your fundamental choice of attitudes. First, let's examine some of the *non*authentic options that are open to our sex-defining freedom.

One of the pillars of existential sex is the clear knowledge that sex is a luxury, not a necessity. Sex is a value that can be freely chosen and not an essence that must be fulfilled. It is a genuine option, not an inevitable obligation; an opportunity, not a duty. One of man's great glories is his freedom to construct himself and his world. It is he—man himself—and neither God nor nature, who assigns the proper role of sex in his lifestyle and world view.

This attitude of choice rather than duty, of freedom rather than obligation, is invigorating and refreshing: It removes the strictures of guilt and opens us up to the spaciousness and grace of our lives. When you realize that the "whether" and the "how" of sex is your own decision, you are truly liberated.

Sex seen as a choice, not a need, frees us from the tyranny of "experts" —moral and medical—returning our bodies and the life of our bodies to the rightful owner: the inwardness residing within each of us.

The existential attitude is a reversal of ordinary ways. If you have integrated into your life the primacy of choice—the centrality of freedom, the ability to invent your own self and your own world (principles A 3 and C 7)—you will not consult the expert to find out what kind of sex life is right or normal. You will instead rest securely on the strength of your freedom.

You will, of course, not make blind or meaningless decisions. The first decision for you as a free person is to discover all you can about your physical possibilities—and *that* is where the experts come in. The experts give you options. Your freedom makes the executive decision. But within your physical and situational limits, the range of free possibilities is refreshingly and inspiringly immense.

How Many Kinds of Sex Are There?

Virtually any definition of sex and its role *can* be a legitimate and authentic choice. However, *all* can also be chosen inauthentically. Authenticity depends on the manner of choice, not the content of choice. The expert in medicine and psychology can tell us what the possibilities are; he can inform us about options. He cannot, however, make the actual choice for us. The expert can tell us what the average individual does or does not do. He cannot tell us, however, whether that average is good or bad, right or wrong, normal or abnormal. Only the freedom of the individual can make that important determination.

What about the philosophic expert—the expert on the nature of man? The philosophic expert cannot tell us the role of sex in life; what he *can* tell us, however, is what the conditions are which make a choice actually undertaken authentic. The characteristics of authentic choice were discussed in Chapter 1. Philosophy does not teach us what is proper sexual behavior. It does teach us what a proper (i.e., authentic) choice is. Thus to the question, "What is better, intercourse or masturbation?" the philosophic expert must answer that the act is neutral. The manner in which the act is chosen determines its authenticity. For a prisoner of war, masturbation may be a healthy physical release; for a man on his honeymoon—where intercourse is the symbol of self-transcendence and love—it may be a sign of failure. Conversely, for a couple in love, intercourse may create deep meanings; in a rape, where there is no mutual consent, intercourse is thoroughly inauthentic. An act in accord with the existentially disclosed nature of man, as embodied in the master table, is authentic. That includes the masturbating prisoner of war and the loving couple in intercourse. On the other hand, an act that is contrary to the nature of man, one which violates the field of consciousness, is always inauthentic, whether it be the masturbating honeymooner or the rapist.

In sum, authenticity means (a) choosing with conscious deliberateness and (b) choosing so as to harmonize with the structure of the field of consciousness, which means one recognizes the ambiguities of life, the need for self-reliance, the capacity for commitment and the other characteristics of the master table. Inauthenticity occurs when either (a) or (b) is violated.

THE GIVEN IN SEX

What is the given or raw datum in sex? This is the element that is unchangeable, unavoidable, absolute, and essential to the larger complex usually called the sexual experience. All experiences—that is, thoughts, perceptions, and feelings—are part given and incontrovertible fact, part interpretation. It is not always easy to separate the two. The given in an experience cannot be changed; about it no error is possible, while interpretations of that experience can be multiple. In the given aspect of an experience there is no freedom. However, in the interpretation of that experience are freedom of definition, freedom of attitude, and freedom of organization. The given is natural, as it were, while the interpreted is learned. Discovering the interpreted aspect of sex is crucial because it discloses to us the full and precise range of freedom that we have with respect to human sexuality.

We can probably agree that the only irrevocable given, uninterpreted, and invariable fact about sex is a specific kind of genital "itch" or a generalized urge of pursuit. Although a clear description of the "pure" sexual urge is difficult, it is not difficult for each individual to recover that element in his experience of sexuality which is irreducible. A person knows when that itch exists and he also knows when that itch has been satisfied. The itch is *given;* it is not open to choice. Our freedom consists in the *attitudes* we take toward that itch.

Superimposed on that physiological given—the pure itch—are two kinds of interpretations: inaccessible and accessible, unfree and free. Inaccessible interpretations are learned, but learned early and learned so thoroughly that the individual seems to have lost all free control over them. Accessible interpretations are social conventions, ideas, and fads.

A good illustration is the difference between homo- and heterosexuality. The sexual itch itself is neutral. It is pure instinct. It can be satisfied in any number of ways: through heterosexual intercourse, through homosexual intercourse, through masturbation, through sodomy and other perversions. However, each individual has his own type of acceptable experience and acceptable gratification of that itch. And even though that mode of gratification (heterosexual intercourse, let us say) is learned and thus interpreted, it is an interpretation of such long standing, and an interpretation so ancient in the history of the individual, that he has lost contact with his freedom of choice over that interpretation. There are, of course, exceptions. People who achieve access to the deepest roots of their freedom can change their reflexes, their habits, and their personality structure completely. But the average person finds that such penetrating search involves more trouble than he wishes. In an absolute sense, then, in the sense of the purely physical nature of man, the mode of gratification is learned, changeable, and thus free. But from the social point of view, that freedom is inaccessible to most people and is thus a kind of social or learned given.

What satisfies is also what arouses. What arouses sexual desire is also learned, but learned early and thoroughly, so that modification is difficult. Nevertheless, the distinction between the physiological given (which is absolute) and the social given (the inaccessible freedom of interpretation) is important. Society can gradually change the second, as women's liberation has tried. But the first is forever resistant to change. Thus, women may be taught early to be submissive to men and less ambitious than men. That pattern is established so early in the development of children that it cannot be readily changed. However, social reformers appear. They cannot shake these old habits in themselves, but they can, through the use of their reason, change the upbringing of their children quite deliberately and consciously and thus create a new generation of women different from their own. But the existence of the pure physiological itch cannot be changed by radical social movements of liberation.

The accessible interpretation of our sexual itch is where we have reasonably free control. Our search for authenticity must begin by exercising our freedom here where we have the most control. We can make free decisions on how to integrate the physiological and social sexual nature into our total life plan. In other words, we are free to choose to accept ourselves as we are, with neuroses, foibles, and all, and make the best of it. That integration is accessible to our freedom. It does not involve depth psychology or behavior modification. This point can be seen in an illustration.

Joel

Joel is a twenty-six-year-old voyeur. He is a waiter in a good restaurant located in the financial district of a large city, one which is frequented by well-dressed secretaries, often with escorts. Joel is an intelligent man, which is his salvation. For him the raw datum of sex, the pure itch, is not different from that of so-called "normal" people. He can get an erection and have an orgasm and then lose the erection.

So much for his absolute or physiological given. But when we now examine the social or inaccessible interpretation which Joel imposes on that primal itch, we recognize that he achieves arousal and gratification in what are considered perverse ways. These perversions are learned re-actions; they are *interpretations* of the meaning of his *given* physical sexual function. These interpretations are in essence free, but Joel has no access any longer to that freedom. Perhaps twenty years ago he did. The social expression of his physiological sexuality is that of an eight-year-old. He has learned to express his sexuality today, at twenty-six, in essentially the same way he did eighteen years ago. His sexual life con-sists in peeping at girls in his restaurant, of increasing his excitement by risking something—his manner of serving is unusually obstrusive, sus-piciously solicitous—and then subsequently in masturbating.

But he is unhappy and understands, intellectually at least, his situa-tion. He wants to change. He must either change his sexual childishness or change the fact that his voyeurism troubles him.

Joel now thinks of his total life. Sex is but one aspect of a total life which includes many additional and different contacts with himself and with the world around him. In the social integration of his sexual life, in his sexual mode of being in the world, Joel is free. He knows he is free and he is willing to put that freedom to full use for the sake of a better life for himself, with reduced anxiety and guilt, one less dominated by his obsession with peeping.

In other words, there is a free aspect to Joel's life, a zone over which he has control and to which he has access. He can learn to accept the perverse socialization of his sexuality. His perversion emanates from a deeper zone of freedom, mostly inaccessible without depth psychotherapy. If his decision is to adjust to his perversity, then he can and must further decide how to gratify his sexuality. For example, he has to decide whether or not to choose a job based on his sexual needs. The demands of his present job are far below his education and ability. He has chosen it for neurotic reasons. Included in Joel's job decision is the broader issue of how important sexuality is to be in his life. Not many people choose their job or profession based on sexual criteria. He must then choose whether or not he is to satisfy his voyeuristic needs at all.

But there are other options open to Joel. One of these is to search for mature ways of heterosexual expression. This is best done through therapy.

When Joel first came to me for philosophical consultation he had essentially three options open—forget, adjust, or change. These options would have the following consequences: (1) Continue with his inauthenticity. Joel's basic lifestyle was one in which guilt over his inadequacy dominated. Also, Joel made sex—his brand of it—far more central to all aspects of his life than does the average heterosexual. Because of his guilt about his voyeuristic adaptation and his overemphasis on the importance of sex in life, Joel was effectively paralyzed in all other areas of his life: personal relations, professional possibilities, and meaning in general. One basic reason for his paralysis was his fear of getting into compromising situations with his customers, that is, of being too obvious (although Joel repeatedly asserted that he needed risk for sexual excitement). He was anxious about being fired. In fact, Joel had frequent anxious fantasies about being arrested. Perhaps unconsciously that is what he wanted.

(2) Joel's second option was to make an adjustment through integration. Joel and I discussed the possibility of adapting his lifestyle to his neurosis. Adjustment through integration would mean that Joel would make a commitment to find some of life's real values and real meanings, such as being of service to others, and that he then choose to integrate his own individual, bizarre sexuality into that larger project for his life.

(3) In the end, however, Joel decided for his third option: To effect a deep change and thus seek a mature expression of his sexual possibilities. He combined the philosophical principles of freedom and of love (C 7 and C 10) with a commitment to analytically oriented psychotherapy—administered by an analytically trained psychiatrist. With remarkable determination and courage, Joel reconstructed his total life project and thereby assisted his body and its responses—that is to say, his automatic sexual reflexes—to continue, at twenty-six, the growth that had been stunted at eight.

ACCESSIBLE AND INACCESSIBLE FREEDOM

The absolute given, then, is the physical sexual urge, the instinct, the itch. The social given or the inaccessible interpretation is the learning and socialization (or absence thereof) that took place early in life. This is the unconscious. The social given is Joel's voyeuristic pattern of meeting his sexual needs. That behavior system can be unlearned, relearned, modified. Furthermore, the social given is also open to social and cultural change, since it is merely a convention. Voyeurism is a perversion because it is an *asocial* way of being sexual.

The conventions of society are a powerful given—both in terms of the strengths of the laws and the weight of social ostracism. The pervert has chosen a countersocial behavior pattern. And it is from the asocial character of his response that he suffers, not from the response itself. Joel's problem is therefore how he can come to terms with the asocial character of his responses. This dilemma he can solve by first placing himself in touch with that part of his lifestyle over which he does have free control.*

Other factors subject to Joel's rational control are (1) decisions regarding business, professional, political, and other "wordly" activities. (2) Finally, the accessible interpreted, the region of conscious freedom, includes for Joel decisions regarding the role of education and therapy in life.

Joel's health depends on how firm a grasp he has on the free interpretation of his sexual dimension. To the degree that he is in possession of his freedom—first his accessible and superficial freedom and later his inaccessible or deeper freedom—he is in command of his life.

In summary, then, there exists in virtually every man and woman a purely physical desire for genital (and general) stimulation and orgasmic release. And that is all there is to sex in any absolute irrevocable sense. That is the only aspect of sex that is not subject to change. We can call this essential element "pure sex" or "basic sex." It has no particular value or "correct" function. All value and function—or social meaning —is a subsequent and reversible interpretation. All value and function are assigned, not given. In this insight lie the answers to the sexual problems of our society.

Let us now look at some possible interpretations of the sexual act *other* than ideal or existential sex.

---

* I once had a female student who, while claiming to be "totally heterosexual," was deeply in love with a homosexual male. Their relationship was good and deep except in sexual matters. (Indeed, there are issues involved in such a relationship that we cannot touch here.) Nevertheless, both were willing to redefine the male-female relationship and the customary social priorities in order to establish a workable life for both of them—together. The couple were willing to expend the effort involved in carrying out these difficult decisions. After three years of marriage they were successful—from the point of view of their own experience and assessment.

7
Interpretations of Basic Sex

According to this definition, sex is like an ugly irremovable wart on one's nose. We must put up with sex as with an incurable illness, learning to live with it but minimizing its influences on us.

Our society certainly does not officially support this view. Not only do social pressures work against whoever holds such a view of sex; medical and psychiatric professionals argue strongly against it as well. Other cultures, however, have openly supported this outlook. In medieval Europe, it was of course common, especially in the monastic orders. In the Orient, the prevalence of asceticism and of the so-called brahmacharya vow (celibacy) supports the rejection of sex. That culture sees overcoming sex as a major triumph, worthy of cosmic and divine rewards. According to a field-of-consciousness theory of man, which gives due emphasis to man's freedom of self-definition, a life of total sexual asceticism can be chosen.

I am not here recommending such a choice, but I am not advising against it either. What matters is that an authentic choice of sexual asceticism is possible, even though our body-focused culture rejects it. Ferdinand's letter given below illustrates this very well. Ferdinand is twenty-four years old.

Three years ago I studied with you. I never said much in class but listened a lot. Your theories have influenced me a great deal. I feel now that I am emotionally strong enough to confess to you how your philosophy has helped with my sexual problem.

While attending your class and unknown to you I was in state prison. I had received special permission to visit your class regularly, as part of my treatment. Every day I attended your class, sir, I had come directly from prison and afterwards I went back directly to prison again. You never knew this, but I was convicted on a sex offense. Since I was sixteen I have been afflicted with a "need for exhibitionism." That's what one of the psychiatrists called it who interviewed me before my trial. Throughout my teens I exhibited my genitals as often as once a week. Each time I told myself it was to be the last time. But my resolve never really worked for long.

On my twentieth birthday I was in a drugstore in Gilroy. I felt a lot of anxiety and a powerful compulsion to exhibit my genitals. As I write this I can clearly visualize my confused feelings. I knew damn well I'd get into a hell of a lot of trouble if I gave in. I exposed myself anyhow. I did it to a woman and two teenage girls who were shopping for Christmas cards and wrapping. A big hysterical scene resulted and I was arrested.

After the arrest I felt strangely reassured and calmed, more so than ever before, when I never had been caught. The arrest was like a resolution to me.

You should know a little of my background. I never saw much of my father. He was mostly drunk or away from home. My mother supported us (she ran a hardware store) and I always admired her strength very much. If it had not been for her our family would have collapsed. In spite of her heavy work load she always had time to take care of my needs. She never forgot a birthday. I know she loves me very much and my arrest and conviction upset her greatly.

While in prison I began to study the world's religions and I came to some important conclusions.

I am hopelessly mixed up sexually. I am a child in sex and will always be one. I also concluded that I was bothered with compulsive needs, like overeating, rather than with pure sex. If I had the choice between a good meal and a sexy girl I'd choose the good meal! In fact, I've never slept with a girl and I don't even think I want to . . . or that it would work out.

Now to get to the point of all this. Two years ago, shortly before my parole, I made the decision to give up sex. You never made that suggestion in your lectures, but it seemed a logical option from your discussion of what you called "man's freedom for self-definition." I applied to the Zen Center in ———— and I spent three months there on a trial basis. I decided to give up thinking of myself as a man in need of sex. I pushed my sexual needs into the background. And I did it not by forcing them there through will power (you used to tell us that this didn't work) but by changing my environment to suit my new choices of self-definition. In so doing I followed your principles.

I know you are going to say that there is a lot more to this situation than meets the eye. Of course, you are right, but, sir, I want you to know one thing: I have never been happier or more at peace in my life. I live in an atmosphere where giving up all sexual desires is made easy; it is encouraged and makes sense. I know if I return to the general world, with its constant stimulation, I will again get confused. I plan, therefore, to devote my life to building and maintaining meditation centers. I left the monastery last year and I am now setting up my own meditation center. Fortunately for me, with the interest in transcendental meditation, that is becoming more and more accepted in the U.S.

*I want you to know, Dr. Koestenbaum, and I write this after months of long
and painful reflection, that I am really reconciled to my being different in the
sexual department. It no longer bothers me and I no longer bother others.*

*What is wonderful about all this is that when I finally was able to choose to
give up sex, or, in your words, to redefine sex as unimportant, my compulsion to
exhibit my genitals, my great anxiety and then relief, seems to have disappeared
permanently. And I believe that my redefinition of myself as a person who will
not respond to his neurotic sexual urges is permanent and easy. I feel a new life is
upon me!*

Sincerely yours,
Ferdinand

SEX IS FRAGMENTED

According to some definitions, sex should be relegated to one region
of life only. Ordinarily, what is called "normal" is really a case of fragmented sex: Sex may have one or a number of functions in life but is
far from all of life or even associated with all of life. A consuming passion
is really an immature lifestyle, according to this interpretation. Let me
illustrate the fragmentation of sex with some case histories.

Robert and Lois

Both Robert and Lois were born and raised on neighboring farms in
the southern part of Minnesota. They married each other in their early
twenties and participated heavily in the various social functions of the
Lutheran Church and in the affairs of their two large families. In their
early thirties they moved to California and changed their lifestyles—in
part deliberately and in part due to the pressures of their new environment. Sex, as discussed in the previous chapter, is the act of intercourse
resulting from an instinctive itch. But what is to be its meaning? Robert
and Lois's social subculture supported a simple two-pronged definition:
Sex is that function which must be performed to produce children.
Children are more important than sex. It is the child-bearing function
of intercourse that gives sex its meaning. Also, sex is the meaning and
proof of marriage. How do you know you are married? In what way is
marriage different from the unmarried state? The answer is in sexual
intercourse. In Robert and Lois's subculture what mattered was that they
were married; that mattered far more than the sexual experience. The
role of sex was to make them feel married. Robert and Lois did not
marry so that they could have sex under accepted conditions. On the
contrary, they had sex so that they would have proof of marriage. "It
was a delight to know you were married," they told me, adding that
"since childhood, we were told we must first marry before we would
be fully accepted in our community and could run our own farm."

After some counseling it became clear that the psychological meaning of their California move was to change their definition of sex as fragmented—a self-concept associated in their minds with Minnesota—to a definition of sex as a total commitment. This they associated with the freer and more experimental attitudes of California.

In other words, Robert and Lois defined the sexual instinct as meaning (1) children and (2) marriage. In this sense, they fragmented their sex lives. But they also recognized their freedom to change from one definition of the meaning of sex to another one.

Glenn

Glenn, who adheres to the *Playboy* philosophy, illustrates a different type of fragmented sex. He is a confirmed bachelor at thirty-two. He lives in a modernistic apartment complex—complete with pools, sauna, tennis courts, recreation room, and golf pro in residence. He drives a Porsche and owns a membership in the European Health Spa. He wears mod clothes and a bushy mustache. Glenn has many pleasures: good music (he prefers late Renaissance compositions and plays the recorder), skiing, movies—and sex. Sex is not a matter of personal relations but the pleasure of two beautiful and tanned bodies enjoying maximum sensuous intensity. Fellatio and cunnilingus have the same critical role in his life as steak and lobster with a glass of chilled rosé. Sex is clearly not part of the meaning of life. In fact, the meaning of life for Glenn is to be as far removed from asking that question as possible. To move with grace and ease from pleasure to pleasure, without attachment and seriousness, that is the meaning of life. Thus, for Glenn, sex means only pleasure —another fragmented view.

Alfred

Alfred illustrates a third type of sexual fragmentation. Alfred is serving a life-sentence for multiple rapes and one murder. He had been an attractive and charming man, not the type commonly associated with criminal behavior. His demeanor was debonair and cultured; to the girls he appeared both rich and loving. However, Alfred suffered from deep anxieties, anxieties which were not expressed, as for most people, through harmless symptoms, but only through the acting out of his conflicts in society. His rapes and the murder were not felt as direct sexual acts at all. They seem to have been compulsive and repetitive efforts to relieve himself of uncontrollable anxiety. His world was dominated by these recurring attacks of anxiety, like an addiction, which he could relieve apparently only through violent acts against women. Moreover, he felt no regret for his assaults. He could therefore not understand why society should punish him as severely as it did.

Alfred in effect defined sex as a vehicle for expressing his aggression socially and as an instrument for relieving his anxiety. That is also a fragmented use of sex. Sex has here been redefined as a crutch for living by an individual who cannot adapt to accepted modes of existence. For him, sex is defined as a substitute or an adjunct, a surrogate for aggression.

The surrogate definition of sex is found any time an individual uses sex to fulfill nonsexual goals. These can be domination, self-respect, escape, aggression, sadism, defense, punishment (of self and other), destruction, buying and selling, or what have you. Most expressions of neurotic or immature sex are less destructive than Alfred's. The man who throws childish temper tantrums in front of his wife or who uses sex to criticize, dominate, or punish his female companion illustrates the same kind of neurotic fragmentation of sex, however.

Anita

Anita's husband is described well in the following letter. Marriage and its sexual aspects mean to him the opportunity to act out childish frustration. He chooses sex as the vehicle through which to exhibit the unfinished business of childhood in his presumably adult relationship. He defines or chooses sex as an instrument for making childish statements.

My husband and I have been married for a year and a half, and by now have resolved many of our conflicts. But ever since I had told him about my past experiences with a black man, he has been totally unable to accept the idea that what I did before we met has no bearing on our future together.

We have gone through counseling, together and separately, and it seems to have helped to the extent that now when he sees a black man and a white girl together he waits until we are alone and are ready to make love before he shuts himself in the bedroom, screams obscenities at me, or slams the door on his way out to get drunk. (I know it may sound ridiculous, but when a twenty-five-year-old man is having a tantrum on the level of a two-year-old, it can be pretty frightening.)

I know that ultimately the decision to accept his self-torture and punishment or demand a divorce will depend on me, but can you suggest any methods of compromise? I have met his anger with frightened silence, indifference and anger on my own part, but nothing really seems to solve the problem. Just lately, when he learned that the black man who is our next-door neighbor had come for a chat with me about school and life in general, he became furiously angry and forbade me to speak to any black person, male or female, again. I'm a twenty-one-year-old adult, raised in a family which does not encourage prejudice—how can I handle this? I really don't want to end our marriage so quickly.

Anita

P.S. My husband comes from a large family of five children; his father died when he was sixteen of a heart attack. Apparently he is very much like his father—nervous, very "picky" about keeping the house clean and orderly, very concerned about his and my weight. He has a terribly anxious attitude about time—time must not be wasted, and one must never be late for even a casual appointment (in this I'm afraid I greatly annoy him, for I just can't seem to be ready exactly on time!). He firmly maintains that he has no prejudicial feelings against blacks, but how on earth could he react so violently if this is true?

Another type of fragmented sex is found in the immature behavior of many teenagers, for whom a sexual experience is not meaningful in itself but necessary for status among their peers. Overtly the young girl relates herself to boys, but the deeper meaning of that relation is addressed to other girls. In this case, sex is chosen to mean prestige.

Opposed to the fragmented approach is existential sex where the sexual project becomes the life project, where life becomes the symbol for sex and its incarnation.

REMEMBER

To summarize the ideas of Chapters 6 and 7:

1. Sex is not necessary for a happy life.
2. To know and to accept the above statement makes sexual fulfillment easier.
3. *You* choose the kind of sex-life you want to lead.
4. You should know your individual bodily and emotional needs.
5. A rational decision is an authentic decision.
6. *Pure* sex, the instinct, is an itch only.
7. *You* choose the *meaning* of that itch as well as the consequences of that choice.
8. All else in your sexual life is your freely chosen *interpretation*.
9. Some of these interpretations are hidden because they come from early childhood, and you can change them only with great difficulty (for instance, "homosexuality").
10. Some of these interpretations are obvious, because they are recent, and you can change them (for instance, "man is always aggressive in sex," "sex means children only").
11. If you have a sexual problem, here are your three ways of responding freely:
    a. Continue your maladjustment. Accept the fact that you are miserable and live with it in peace.
    b. Reorganize your life rationally and intelligently so as to avoid trouble and enhance your strengths.
    c. Make an existential choice: Make a serious commitment to try to change your early childhood sexual conditioning.

EXERCISES

Write *two* short essays on "My interpretation of the meaning of sex." In the first essay discuss your ideal of sex and in the second essay your actual sexual life.

Discuss the essays with a trusted friend.

8

Test Yourself

What Kind of a Lover Are You?

Before reading the following chapters on existential sex you should test yourself. In this way the existential concepts will have greater meaning to you. The test is good preparation for understanding the ideas of existential sexuality. Many of the questions are used to compare your ability to love sexually with those of others who have been measured. Before you look at the scoring technique take the test. Then turn to Appendix B.

Answer the following questions to get an intuitive and approximate measure of the sexualization of your nature. Involved here is not your overt sexual activity (or its absence) but the extent to which your personality understands and is suited to experience sex existentially and authentically. In short, the test might begin to answer for you the question "Do you or would you make a good sexual lover?" Be extremely honest with yourself in your answers. The test is a teaching device, not a psychometric instrument.

If for you a statement is true, circle the T. If it is false, circle F. In some instances you will have to choose between item A and item B.

SCORE

_____	T F	1. In my relation to the opposite sex, I usually play roles and games.
_____	T F	2. I find it difficult to be natural and relaxed when I am with a member of the opposite sex.
_____	T F	3. Love and sex are the most important experiences in life for me.
_____	T F	4. I would like to center my life around sex and love.

_____ T F   5. When I think of sex I automatically think of the relation between two people, not of myself alone.

_____ T F   6. I am a prisoner of my sexual feelings.

_____ T F   7. If I wanted to, I could give up sex.

_____ T F   8. I have a reasonably good understanding of the field-of-consciousness theory of man.

_____ T F   9. I am capable of loving in an emotional and spiritual sense.

_____ T F   10. I find it difficult to accept the love and the affection of another.

_____ T F   11. It is not easy for me to express affection openly and physically.

_____ T F   12. I like my body.

_____ T F   13. I feel comfortable being my body.

_____ T F   14. I secretly wish my body were different.

_____ T F   15. I enjoy physical activity.

_____ T F   16. I don't like to participate in sports.

_____ T F   17. Too many of the important decisions of my life are made for me by other people or by circumstances over which I have no control.

_____ T F   18. I usually make the important choices in my life on my own and by myself.

_____ T F   19. I myself have chosen the values which guide my life.

_____ T F   20. I find it difficult to look another person straight in the eye.

_____ T F   21. I am generally fearful.

_____ T F   22. I tend to be confident.

_____ T F   23. I suffer from anxieties.

_____ T F   24. I am a happy person.

_____ T F   25. I am fastidious about my personal appearance.

_____ T F   26. It is important for me always to be well dressed.

_____ T F   27. I religiously do exercises to keep my body in shape.

_____ T F   28. I am a compulsive person.

_____ T F   29. I "lose my cool" under pressure.

_____ T F   30. The idea of getting a massage pleases me.

_____ T F   31. I lead a mostly sedentary life.

_____ T F   32. I have a great deal of will power.

_____ T F   33. It is important to me to be on a diet.

_____ T F   34. I consider myself to be very organized and efficient in running my life.

_____ T F   35. I am self-conscious about my body.

_____ T F   36. Plastic surgery should be used more widely than it is; plastic surgery is a good tool for making people more attractive.

_____ T F   37. My work is boring and dull.

_____ T F   38. I enjoy my work.

_____ T F   39. If I have a choice, I prefer _making_ a thing rather than _buying_ it.

_____ T F   40. My life is full of deadlines and other pressures.

_____	T F	41. I read the fashion pages (male or female) of magazines.
_____	T F	42. What others think of me is very important to me.
_____	T F	43. I frequently look at myself in a mirror.
_____	T F	44. I like acting or performing before an audience.
_____	T F	45. I often let myself be used by others.
_____	T F	46. (Men) I wash my hair with handsoap, that is, I use no special shampoos.
		(Women) I use relatively little makeup.
_____	T F	47. I believe that my body is ugly.
_____	T F	48. Men who lose their hair should wear hairpieces.
_____	T F	49. Women should wear wigs as soon as their hair begins to thin out.
_____	T F	50. *Playboy* and similar magazines have made a constructive contribution to improving the sexual lives of modern men and women.
_____	T F	51. Knowledge of the erogenous zones of the body is needed in order to have good sexual experiences.
_____	T F	52. Everyone should read a sex manual before marriage.
_____	T F	53. I find nudism embarrassing.
_____	T F	54. I often feel a tightness about the neck.
_____	T F	55. The muscles in my stomach area are frequently stiff and tense.
_____	T F	56. I feel at home in my social environment.
_____	T F	57. I love nature.
_____	T F	58. I am lonely much of the time.
_____	A B	59. This dot represents a bullet; ●. Your first impression is that (A) the bullet is moving *toward* you or (B) the bullet is moving *away* from you.
_____	T F	60. I have bad posture.
_____	A B	61. In selecting a pet I have the choice of a turtle or a rabbit. I choose (A) the rabbit, (B) the turtle.
_____	A B	62. I have the choice of imagining a bear moving *toward me* or moving *away from me.* I choose to visualize the bear (A) as moving *away* from me; (B) as moving *toward* me.
_____	A B	63. Imagine that as you walk you reach a mountain. (A) The mountain stops your progress. (B) The mountain is an invitation to climb it.
_____	A B	64. Imagine a closed door. (A) It is locked; (B) it is not locked.
_____	A B	65. In your fantasy, you are held up by a criminal and he points a gun at you demanding your wallet. (A) You give him your wallet. (B) You fight back.
_____	A B	66. Most people feel that the center of their consciousness is in their head. Now imagine that this center has dropped to the base of your spine, that is, the seat of your pelvic region. (A) It is rather easy for me to imagine that; (B) it is very difficult for me to imagine that.
_____	T F	67. I have decided that I will not use a sexual partner as a mere sex object.

_____	T F	68. In sex I can be so completely involved with my partner that I am truly oblivious to everything else in the world.
_____	T F	69. I think that being the passive partner in sex can really be enjoyed only by the female.
_____	T F	70. I feel that the male should always be the active partner in sex.
_____	T F	71. I believe that a man can enjoy being passive in sex.
_____	T F	72. In sex, the body of my partner should be a symbol for the whole world.
_____	T F	73. I can see no useful connection between religion and sex.
_____	T F	74. In art, the nude body often represents the universe.
_____	T F	75. I love poetry.
_____	A B	76. (A) I deserve love; (B) I do not deserve love.
_____	T F	77. The idea that in sex a woman "surrenders" herself is outdated.
_____	T F	78. I would like to be a nudist.
_____	T F	79. I believe that as a rule of thumb it is better that intercourse be reserved for married people.
_____	T F	80. I believe that society should be completely permissive sexually.
_____	T F	81. Impotence and frigidity can be cured with practice and by using appropriate sexual techniques.
_____	T F	82. Even though many would prefer to think otherwise, sex is truly beautiful only between two physically attractive people.
_____	T F	83. If I should live to be eighty, I think I will be too old for sex.
_____	T F	84. To a contemporary person, the use of perfume is really superfluous for sexual fulfillment.
_____	T F	85. In a beautiful woman, her buttocks are more sexually attractive than her stomach.
_____	T F	86. Knowledge of erogenous zones is very helpful in achieving orgasm.
_____	T F	87. Sex is best at night, because it is a good idea to go to sleep after an orgasm.
_____	TOTAL SCORE	

9
Existential Sex
The Meaning of Body Authenticity

THE DECISION FOR EXISTENTIAL SEX

Now we are going to discuss how existential philosophy or the field-of-consciousness personality theory can help a couple achieve enhanced sexual fulfillment. The preliminaries are now established:

1. The decision to make life sexual is freely made by two independent persons. The sexualization of life is neither good nor bad. It has natural consequences, just as the rejection of total sex has natural consequences. (Total sex, or existential sex, is the organization of life around the concept and experience of sexuality.) Each individual chooses his relation to sex, with the attendant consequences. In choosing total sex, he rejects other values. In denying total sex, he makes room for these additional values but loses the rewards of total sex.

2. Although serious, the decision for the total sexualization of life has a game quality because while the decision for pansexualism is enjoyable, it can also be stopped or changed. The couple knows that they are not condemned to be sexual, they are not helplessly overcome by sexual passion; they have freely chosen the sexualization of their lives. Even the individual who is "overcome" by sexual passion has *chosen* to permit these feelings to well up within him and has *chosen* to expose himself to a sexually stimulating environment, which will affect the feelings that arise within him. Consequently, the organization of life around sex is a freely chosen constitution of our world (theme A 3 of the master table).

62

3. The basic principle of existential sex is the decision to create a lifestyle and a relation between the male and female that conforms to and is expressive of the fundamental characteristics of human existence as disclosed by a field-of-consciousness personality theory. This theory emphasizes the reality of our consciousness and its continuity with the world. Existential sex can be called a pansexualism, because the physiological sexual encounter is chosen to become the paramount metaphor in the life of man.

4. Finally, the existential characteristics stressed in existential sex are a translation of the phenomenon of encounter—as discussed in the chapters on existential love—in sexual foreplay and sexual intercourse.

Let me explain. In discussing existential sex I begin by recalling the elements of existential or ideal love, which define the kind of interpersonal encounter that I call a transcendental relationship. I then suggest ways in which that ideal of conscious love can be expressed physically; I try to show how a conscious encounter can be translated into physical and biological reality. That is the existential secret of supreme sexual gratification.

The *first* (of nine) characteristic of authentic sex is full embodiment, which I call "body authenticity." Body authenticity can be achieved by recognizing three of its components: playing the game of "no-game," being the body-subject, and living from the inside out.

Play the Game of "No-Game"

The decision for authentic sex is first of all the decision to avoid roles. If we play no roles but just let ourselves be, we feel the continuity of consciousness with the body. That is one facet of body authenticity. To decide to play the game of no-game is the decision to live from the inside out, to radiate from the center, to take one's cue for life's values from the center and not from the outside, from the periphery. Authentic sex is the decision to play the role of no-role, to create the game of no-game out of the richness of life's potential.

We can sometimes tell by a person's appearance whether or not he is living a no-game existence, a life that moves from the inside out. The gaze of the no-game person often is uninterrupted, confident, straight, steady, and direct, whereas the gaze of the game person—he who lives from the outside in—can be furtive, evasive, and broken. The game person or compulsive role-player permanently scans his surroundings, like a cornered fox, to test for signals and cues, for approval and rejection. He is ready to respond—and only to respond—within the second. He only reacts; he never acts.

BE THE BODY-SUBJECT

A person who lives from the inside out is not likely to care much about his physical appearance. In short, he is not self-conscious. The reason is that he lives *through* his body. This is the second component of body authenticity. The person with body authenticity exists inside his body and is no more aware of the body than a person who always wears glasses is aware of them. A good racing driver feels the tires touching the road as an extension of himself. He experiences his car from the inside out—he does not see it as a spectator would. The body of the person who lives from the inside out is the vehicle that carries him from the inside of his consciousness to the outside that is the world. He does not view his body through the eyes of another. He lives his body so that his body becomes the subjective center. His body does not become the object of perception or inspection. This person is authentic. One can tell this authenticity from his casual and relaxed physical appearance: healthy, but not compulsively or artificially so.

One consequence of the insight that authenticity is living from the inside out—important to teachers in physical education and recreation—is that all bodily exercises must be enjoyable and never forced. Sports, hiking, dancing, massage, and similar physical activities must be experienced as thoroughly pleasurable and enjoyable. Exercising must be an integral part of one's style of life, not a fragmented extra sandwiched between busy sedentary moments in the office, at the plant, or in the conference room. It is thus a mistake to look upon physical exercise as based on will power. The person who is authentically physical in his being-in-the-world will enjoy his body as the vehicle for life itself. He will not shape his body—like a piece of clay or marble—with exercises and diets for the sake of appearance or artificial standards. He will live his body.

If you believe man is only an organismic thing rather than also a subjective inward consciousness, it does make sense to use will power to shape the body. It does make sense to treat your body like a well-run factory. A successful modern man can have his car serviced with minimum inconvenience to himself: He can also service his body through short-cuts to exercise. But there is something highly artificial and unsatisfactory in this approach to the human body. Let us assume that efficiency and will power *do* work: We have fashioned bodies into good shape. Now what?

Man is a consciousness as well as a body, and consciousness is continuously connected with the world; the body is the organ of consciousness, and the body is the instrument which moves the inner consciousness to the world beyond. If you believe this, then a sense of continuity and unity with the body develops, a feeling of brotherhood and love with the world, of simplicity and ease in living. A sense of rightness about the universe appears as a result of this field-of-consciousness theory of man.

The bodily life is the life of the body-subject. The world is experienced through the body; the body itself is not experienced. The body is the finger that touches, the eye that scans, and the ear that hears the world. The body is not itself what is seen, heard, or touched. That is the meaning of the body-subject.

A person who lives bodily celebrates life through the body. For many, to live bodily means a total change in lifestyle. As a rule, diets and exercise programs leave no permanent results. Most individuals retain their basic personality structures indefinitely. Diet and exercise programs fail because they are based on the use of will power which, in turn, is based on the ghost-in-a-machine theory of man. Will power manipulates the body from shape A (flabby) to shape B (firm) or from shape X (fat) to shape Y (thin). Will power does not *live in* the body but *looks at* the body from outside. Only a change in one's self-concept will lead to a real change in one's life.

Modern life tends to be sedentary and mechanized. The new life is a return to the truth of the body. And the truth of the body is that it is a body-subject, *not* a body-thing or a body-object. The truth of the body is living bodily, as, for example, in the agricultural life, fishing and hunting; it is the life in the water, in the mountains, and in the snow. It is the life of joy in movement and of pleasure in physical exertion. The sedentary nature of our society is the enemy of the natural man. We have built machines to do our physical living for us and we are now paying the price for it with destruction of the environment and neglect of the body. The life of the body is one of enjoyment rather than efficiency.

A man must enjoy his work, not the completion of it. If all he cares for is completion, his work is drudgery and the product is sloppy. If he lives his work, the product is excellent and the completion almost unnoticed.

The bodily life is a life of inner time, a life of relaxation. Stresses and pressures imposed by external time schedules, deadlines, and efficiency experts are foreign to the bodily life.

LIVE FROM THE INSIDE OUT

A person who looks "pretty" or narcissistic lives from the outside in. He is excessively fastidious and self-conscious. He strives to be the exact replica of pictures and styles in the latest fashion magazines. The "pretty" person has abdicated his center to others and perceives himself exclusively through their eyes. The real center of a "pretty" individual is dead. His surrogate center is the artificial standards of current fashion and the arbitrary norms of self-styled "experts." Others *use* him rather than meet and respect him. Appearance is all-important, so diets, exercises, mirrors, hairpieces, cosmetics, and fashionable clothes become crucial.

An unattractive or "ugly" person is likely to live from the outside in. Examples are a masculine-looking female, an effeminate male, an ill-kempt, dirty, and smelly person, and a vastly overweight or dangerously underweight individual. These are all conditions which, unlike crippling, are often the result of personality structures and thus are avoidable: They are thus the result of human freedom. The "pretty" person views his body as an object and molds it according to some artificial and external standard. A similar act of self-creation is performed by the "ugly" person. The latter differs from the former in that the ugly one has as his external object-model a self-concept of derision, neglect, failure, and self-punishment, rather than one of vainglory. Since their centers are external to themselves, neither the "pretty" nor the "ugly" person is capable of authentic bodily being.

It follows that both the "pretty" and the "ugly" person are incapable of good authentic sex, for the roots of sexual inadequacy must be sought in the degree to which an individual's personality structure does or does not conform to the subject-to-object field-of-consciousness theory of man. The "pretty" and the "ugly" individuals have their centers where the world should be and have thus distorted completely the growth process of human existence.

To achieve authentic sex, neither manipulating the body through improved techniques nor stimulating your partner through novel positions is effective. A shift of self-concept is required. If you can live from the inside out, become the body-subject, and play the game in which all games and roles are abandoned—the game of no-game—you can experience ideal existential sex. You can then express the meaning of life and of love sexually.

REMEMBER

1. Existential or ideal sex is not a need, not a natural condition, but a free choice.
2. The decision for authentic sex is the decision to live through your body.
3. In body authenticity we live spontaneously and play no games.
4. In body authenticity we are not self-conscious.
5. Your body is the ego.
6. In body authenticity we live from the inside out.

The tests that follow can help you assess the extent of your bodily authenticity. They are informal and interpretation of the results is intuitive. The goal is to provoke discussion and insight.

10

Existential Sex
Exercises for Body Authenticity

Exercise 1: Body Observation Test

This test is designed to get you acquainted with your body and to let your body and its dress tell you whether you are celebrating life with and through your body (which is authentic) or whether you are an observer of your body and model it after an externally established standard (which is inauthentic).

This experiment can be carried out alone or together with a member of the opposite sex, one with whom you already have established a love relationship or with whom you have decided to establish one. The exercise of course has different meanings if performed alone from those it would have if performed in an encounter situation. If you perform the exercise with another person, then you must view it as sexual foreplay. You become aware of each other's body. You focus in unusual ways on each other's body and you can help each other to enhance *being* rather than *observing* your own bodies. Many couples have found this activity highly pleasurable and exciting, as well as conducive to significant emotional growth.

In this exercise you are asked to view yourself in a full-length mirror under four different conditions: (1) as you arise in the morning; (2) as you are dressed to start your daily routine, the kind of routine that defines who you are in society (job, school, housework); (3) as you are dressed to go to an important appointment, that is to say, the conditions that elicit the highest role you have set for yourself, the role you are in when you

67

wish to make a good impression; and (4) totally naked, as you are when your roles and robes have been shed. In addition, you or your partner could take a color photograph of your body under these four circumstances for purposes of further implementing this exercise.

When finished, you will have considerable and sensitive raw material to analyze and discuss. New and strange feelings will have been aroused. Here are some questions to be considered:

1. How did you react emotionally to the exercise? Your reactions will of course be stronger if you perform your exercise in front of a witness rather than alone. Nevertheless, the *type* of reaction may be the same and if you train yourself to be sensitive to subtle shades of feelings, this exercise can be performed successfully alone.

If you were greatly bothered by it (or, for that matter, greatly pleased), chances are you are overly self-conscious. That probably means your body is to you primarily an object that is seen rather than a life that is lived. Your body does not conform (or conforms gorgeously) to an external model and you feel inadequate and inferior (or splendid and superior). You are inauthentic. On the other hand, if you were not much bothered (or indifferent to the possibility of being pleased), even when your partner took your picture stark naked, you are probably authentically living unself-consciously *through* your body. Your body is your way of living in this world; it is not an object with whose appearance you are constantly concerned. In this case you use your body to live; you do not need to remake it into an ideal object so that others can praise you for it. If, for example, you see your father or your mother in your body, you can ask yourself if that pleases or displeases you. Any excessive reaction—positive or negative—will tend to be inauthentic. The authentic response is one of indifference, of not attaching much anxiety to the manner of appearance.

If your reaction to performing the test was inauthentic, use this exercise to retrain your mode of being in the world; repeat the exercise with the determination to not be troubled or pleased. Try to remain indifferent. At least try to capture the feeling of being indifferent to your body's appearance—imagine what that feeling would be like. You should proceed as follows: Imagine that you really do not care how your body looks— beautiful or ugly. If you can imagine that clearly in your fantasy for even five minutes, you will have made progress towards bodily authenticity.

The ultimate reality of your body authenticity is what you think and how you feel; the truth about your body authenticity is the fundamental manner in which you exist in this world. These are attitudes, perceptions and decisions and not actual physical characteristics. Here is good news, because you can achieve control over attitudes, perceptions and decisions far more easily than you can remake your body. The message here is the reassuring fact that those things that matter most (attitudes) are in your own hands. The mistaken belief that fate (for instance, the shape of our faces) determines our happiness can now be confidently abandoned.

2. *Now imagine that the person in the mirror and the photograph is* not *you.* In fact, imagine that it is someone you have never seen before. Write down your detailed impressions of that person. Would you hire him if you were an employer? Would you want that person for a friend? Would you trust him? respect him? believe him? Do you have contempt for him? Of whom does he remind you? Are you happy or upset about the discovered resemblance? Is that person in the mirror or in the photograph successful? Is he happy? How long will he live?

As you answer these questions a picture of body authenticity emerges. You must analyze the private meanings of your answers. They tell you how you exist in this world. They tell you something very fundamental about the self-concept working within you. Once that self-image (not the one you would *like* to have, but the one which actually seems to be at work within you) is explicitly out in the open, you have control over it. You control your self-image if you are conscious of it; your self-image controls you if it is unconscious. You can now ask yourself whether that self-image is one of body authenticity. If it is, then you are ready for authentic sex. If it is not, then you must first change that self-concept to an authentic one before you can lead a life of existential sex.

3. *Make the assumption that your body describes your life-style.* Your body is the accumulation of all the living that you have done. Your body is the storehouse for all your memories; it is a map of all your past decisions and choices, which are still at work today. Then check items such as your hair, your manner, if any, of shaving (whether male *or* female). Check those muscles that appear to be overdeveloped and those that are flabby. Look for dominant regions. Examine the distribution of your weight in your body. Also, analyze the appropriateness of the clothes you wear. Study your face. If you were to meet a stranger who had your face, what do you think it tells you about him? Observe the lines in your face. Look for any tight muscles and for distortions. What do you think these features say about your body's life?

Now try to be as imaginative and as explicit as you can in translating these physical memories into words. Describe the psychology of your body. Describe how your body exists in the world around it. Describe the life your body has led and the decisions it has made not on the basis of what you remember, but of what you see as you study your body in the four poses suggested.*

Having done all of the work requested above, preferably as dialogue,

---

* The above procedure is succinctly summarized in the following quotation, taken from an interview with Stanley Keleman (*Psychology Today,* September, 1973, page 65):

> My first interest is in a person's body presence. I look to see how much co-ordination and grace there is in the body, where it is weak or rigid, what parts are overdeveloped or have too little development, how much vitality is obvious. And I try to locate the physical and psychic constrictions that have become habitual.

conversation, in writing or on tape, go over it and ask yourself (or discuss with your partner) the final question:

4. How authentic is your being a body? Make a final evaluation. How smooth and natural is the flow of your consciousness into your body and through to the world? Are you generally unaware of the fact that you have a body? Do you use your body to live *in* the world and *with* people? Or do you use your body to escape from the world, to run away from others and even from your own consciousness? For example, does your body look as if your head (the traditional locus of consciousness) is integrated easily with your will and feelings (chest) and your more primitive functions of defecation and sexuality (pelvic region)? Do head, chest, and pelvis seem as if they belong together and function well in unison? Or do they seem that they were assembled artificially and do not belong in one unitary and smoothly functioning system? It would help you now to examine your neck muscles: Are they stiff, tight? Are they loose, relaxed? How is your spine? Your back? What does your neck tell you about the connection between your head (consciousness) and the rest of your nature (torso)? Does your pelvic region seem integrated with the rest of your torso, or do you observe a blocking tightness interfering with a sense of unity?

You can now examine the relation of your limbs to your body. Your arms are for reaching and getting close, but also for defense and protection. Where are your arms? What seems to be their function in *your* body? Do they bring you closer to the world or do they keep the world away from you? The same questions can be asked about your legs.

With some practice you will find this exercise useful and not difficult.

EXERCISE 2: PROJECTION TEST

Another good way to discover your body's being-in-the-world and to check for body authenticity is to examine your projections on ambiguous stimuli. Gather a series of ambiguous shapes, photographs, and pictures—or construct your own. Look for quick reactions from you to these ambiguous data.

Materials which you can use include professional projective tests, such as the Rorschach, Holtzmann, and TAT. But these are difficult to get; you can experiment making your own inkblot cards. Use black ink or, even better, several colors of ink. Drop it (with a dropper) on the center of a card or a large sheet of paper. Fold the card. Open the card. Let dry. Select those inkblots that seem to lend themselves to a variety of projections and discard the others.

If you don't like inkblots, you can probably find some reproductions of modern art which are good for the purpose of projection. You can also use clouds and other unusually and ambiguously shaped natural objects.

Your task (and that of your partner, if you have one) is now to develop a series of reactions to these ambiguous pictures. What do you see in them? What do they look like? Do you see animals or people? Do you recognize the people? What movement do you find in your projective interpretations? What movements and what emotions are associated with the objects? You would, for example, associate a different emotion with a fresh rose than with a deep cave. Let your fantasy run free and record your responses.

You are now ready to analyze your responses. Look for patterns in your responses and compare these patterns with those of others. In particular, you should look for clues to movement, pointing, and direction. Are you moving *into* the picture (possible authenticity) or *away from* the picture (possible inauthenticity)? Is the object or landscape inviting (authentic) or uninviting (inauthentic)? Does the object move or point away from you (authentic)? Toward you (inauthentic)?

The criteria for authenticity are based on one simple consideration. If the projection points from your actual lived center to the outer world, then the automatic projection conforms to the nature of man as assumed in the field-of-consciousness theory of man. Let us assume that the datum is a mere point: "•" Some extreme projections are that the point is an arrow, a dart, or a bullet. Projection 1 is that the bullet (or arrow, or dart) moves towards you, the observer. Projection 2 is that the bullet is moving away from you, into space. There are of course innumerable other projections possible, but let us concentrate on these two simple ones. Projection 2 would be interpreted as probably authentic because the movement implicit in the projection conforms to the outward and self-transcending nature of consciousness in the field-of-consciousness theory of man. This fact is evident especially from the master table themes A 1 and C 13. The projection is an inside-out experience. Projection 1, on the other hand, reverses the outward and emerging vector that is the consciousness which radiates from the human center, and that projection would imply an inauthentic way of organizing the experience of space. Projection 1 is an outside-in experience.

Do not pay too much attention to individual responses. Only general patterns are significant and these have definite meaning only if you can compare them to the responses of others. If you are living from the inside-out, which is essential to body authenticity, you are likely to see that pattern repeated in your instinctive projections. Conversely, if you live from the outside-in, then that vector is likely to be reflected in the pattern of your projections.

If you feel comfortable living from the inside-out, then you are also likely to experience your body as a living subject (that is, the body-subject) rather than an observed object. Also, if your projection patterns are predominantly inside-out, then, in all probability, you are not a compulsive role- or game-player, but feel at ease with no role and no game at all.

Should this test indicate that you feel inauthentic in these areas, your projection test can also become an exercise for self-development. Try to *control* your projections. Make the effort to regulate what you perceive. Make an effort to *change* your projections.

For example, to Kate, who went through this series of projection exercises in one of my workshops, a certain black and white inkblot looks like a skeleton. She said that the skeleton faced her, looked at her, and threatened to move towards her. Kate had an outside-in, that is, an inauthentic response. Now, deliberately, Kate tried to reverse the inward-pointing direction that is the underlying pattern of her projective response. She tried to visualize the skeleton as moving away from her. Then she tried to look *between* the bones of the skeleton—the openings—to the world beyond, to the other side, and imagine what might be there in the distance. Finally, she tried to change the skeleton into something else—a task that proved difficult for her: With some effort, it did manage to become the smoke or the trail of a rocket that had just been shot out into space! Kate repeated this exercise a number of times and discovered that her newly acquired outward-moving habit carried over to other activities as well. She reported that she walked differently, faster, with more determination and more erect.

EXERCISE 3: GUIDED FANTASY TEST

In this exercise you develop daydream fantasies that could give you a clue about the direction and movement that your consciousness tends to take. For example, start by imagining a field. Now describe it carefully. Next, analyze it for freedom and direction of movement. Are *you* in the meadow? If so, are you moving or static? How easy and natural is it for you to place yourself in the image of the daydream field, and how easy is it for you to move within it? Furthermore, what do you see beyond the field? More open space (authentic)? Mountains that invite climbing (authentic)? Rugged cliffs that imprison or protect (inauthentic)? Dark and ominous woods with high trees? a fence (both inauthentic)?

Another useful fantasy is to imagine an animal—at a zoo or coming out of a cave, scurrying in the desert or grazing on the meadow, appearing in a jungle or at your window. Now examine the inherent mobility of the animal (for instance, cheetah *vs.* turtle). Also study what it is doing and what you can make it do in your fantasy. A bear may approach you (inauthentic). You may see a horse, mount it, and ride forth on it (authentic).

The guided fantasy test will often tell you rather clearly where you stand in body authenticity, in the sense that crucial to body authenticity is the automatic tendency to move from within the deepest depth of your consciousness out onto the inviting and responsive world. If your fantasies refuse to move in this direction then we can assume a degree of alienation and inauthenticity in your mode of being-in-the-world. That is to say, the field of consciousness is not expressed in your body; you have not yet achieved body authenticity.

You can also use this exercise to practice body authenticity. That is accomplished by coercing fantasies in the desired directions: Practice imagining open fields, open seas, flying birds, etc., and move with these vectors. The fantasy, as you become accustomed to it, will leave its mark in your reality. The carryover tends to be significant. The use of guided daydreams is often called "therapy without insight."

EXERCISE 4: WORD ASSOCIATION TEST

For this test you select a list of words that could be either moats or bridges, fences or paths; that is, words which designate objects or conditions that could be interpreted either as obstacles to further movement and direction or as possibilities for facilitating self-transcendence. You think of objects that are both blocks and shields on the one hand—dissociating and breaking connections—and pathways or doors, openings towards unification, on the other. As before, what counts is not only individual answers but patterns and comparisons with the responses of others.

Here is a list of ambiguous words that has been found useful: fence, border or boundary, cage, bars, river, lake, sea, ocean, mountain range, cliff, precipice, stairs, bedsheets, gravity, door, lock, horse, automobile, airplane, etc. In connection with each word (and others you can think of) ask yourself whether your predominant association is (1) that the object keeps you out, holds you back, stops you, frightens you and you acquiesce; or (2) that the object is an invitation to move beyond, to transcend, to expand, to move outward. In terms of patterns, the first is likely to be inauthentic and the second, authentic.

As before, you can turn this test into a practice exercise by controlling your associations. Frequently, a person can successfully modify his emotional responses by changing his fantasies. This exercise is not easy but can be very effective.

Authentic or existential sex is predicated on a person's fully developed ability to be a physical body. We have been focusing on the existential theme of self-transcendence, the fact that man is time and that man is the emergent movement from subjective consciousness to outermost world. The master table illustrates these points through themes A 1, C 12 and C 13.

Exercise 5: How to Be Centered

A final presentation of the meaning of body authenticity can be established by developing a sense of the centeredness and the unity of the human being. In existential sex, the body represents even more than the universe in that it represents all of being—the sacred and the profane, the real and the ideal, the mental and the material, the cosmic as well as the inward. Certain specific metaphors are either obvious or have become codified over the millennia of human history: The head is pure consciousness, the chest is the will and the seat of most feelings, and the pelvis is the region of man's subterranean passions.

Two aspects of this metaphor are of particular importance: "Where is the center (or, where is the experience of the center)?" and "Are there any blocks preventing the unity and the connectedness of these three parts?"

In our abstract and conceptual culture, the center is often in the head. This is bodily and thus sexual alienation. The most distant region from that conscious center of the head is the pelvic region. The id, the functions of sex and defecation, located in the pelvis, are thus the object-pole of human experience. A life structure with our center in the head is adequate for the *understanding* of existential sex, but not for its living. In order to live existential sex, the center must be lowered to the bottom of the spine, to the seat of man—to the point that in yoga is called the Kundalini.

Since we are here dealing with experiences and not concepts, it is important that you and I endeavor to experience the lowering of the center. One simple procedure is to imagine that the seat of your awareness, the center of your person, is at the point at which the spine terminates. Imagine the seat of the spine to be the center of the sunburst that is your field of consciousness. Experience waves of self-transcendence radiating from that center and warming the rest of your pelvic region. You can feel waves of glowing energy move upward and forward from that point at the base of your spine where you have now located the center of being itself. You can perceive the world from the point of view of the pelvic region. In that case, a sense of touch, movement, and radiating energy replaces the field of vision of head-centered individuals. Such a fantasy can arouse strong sexual feelings before any other regions of the body (i.e., chest and head or will and reason) are consulted or referred to. But authentic sex begins with a kiss rather than with coitus, which means that the sense of energy must first move from the base of the spine through the entire body all the way up to the mouth and the lips before authentic sex becomes possible. As the energy moves in this fashion several important aspects of body authenticity emerge.

First, the energy is sexual: It has its origin in the pelvic region and it moves first and foremost to the genital region. Second, the center remains at the base of the spine. The upward movement of energy in body authenticity is not like the movement of a ball but like the spreading of a small fire into a massive conflagration. The center remains in the seat, but its radiations fill the entire body. Third, the upward movement is not along the spine alone. On the contrary, it is along the exposed and softer tissues in the front of the body—the belly and stomach, the chest with its heart and lungs, the breast, and so forth.

Fourth, and perhaps most important of all, it is very common to find blocks or shields preventing *both* this upward movement of the pelvic radiations *and* the initial downward movement of the center from between the eyes in the head to the base of the spine in the pelvis. The usual places for these shields—evidenced by cramped and tight muscles—are in the areas of the neck and the waist (or stomach or diaphragm). A person who experiences these obstacles in the free and voluntary downward relocation of his center suffers from blocks in his body, which are the same as blocks in the field of consciousness. Similarly, the person who finds parts of his being shielded from the waves emanating upwards and forward from the pelvic region has created obstacles in the path of his unity, wholeness, continuity, and integration. He is fragmented. These blocks can often be broken directly and physically, as through strong massage and by directly handling the muscles involved.

The philosophic underpinning of body authenticity is that the body is a metaphor for the fundamental structure of being itself. What in fact happens in cases of inauthentic sex is that the field of consciousness is interrupted. The field referred to in master table theme A 1 has lost its natural character. That interruption is "incarnated," as it were, in symbolic blocks in the neck or waist or stomach region of the body. Similarly, the center of the field of consciousness is—in its philosophical purity—not a bodily place at all. However, that center can be symbolically located in the body. And body authenticity means that this location is moved from the head (between the eyes, an inch or so inside the skull) to the seat of the spine.

(My term for the use of the body as symbol for being itself is "cathexis." That point is made in theme C 9 of the master table.)

An exercise that I have found effective in my work is to adopt a yoga upside-down posture, with legs slightly bent towards the head so as to give maximum prominence to the pelvic region. Once a comfortable balance has been achieved, the individual should engage in a fantasy in which he gradually moves his center to the seat of the spine and then allows it to grow. The pelvis now occupies the place which in the upright posture of man is usually assigned to the head. The relocated center—as it did before when it was in the head—will gradually expand by dropping down of its own weight through the front of the body toward the head. In this exercise I take advantage of the metaphors of "high" and "upward" commonly associated with the center in our head-oriented culture. I try to fool our system of metaphors.

We are now ready to move on to aspects of ideal or existential sex other than body authenticity.

11

Full Embodiment in Therapy

As was discussed in Chapter 9 and 10, body authenticity is the full act of embodiment; it is the decision to be the body and to live through the body. It is the decision to define the body and its life as representing in one gargantuan poetic metaphor the total field of consciousness that is being. And body authenticity is the *sine qua non* for the full sexualization of human existence. It is important to remember, however, that I do not espouse a hedonistic naturalism or an animalistic or organismic world view. I am simply asserting that while an ascetically detached and saintly, mystical life style is a definite existential possibility, the sexualization of life presupposes that the conscious center freely identifies itself with (cathects) the body.*

In this chapter I will explore the relation between consciousness and the body as seen from the point of view of an existential theory of man and consider its applications to an existentially oriented therapy.

AUTHENTIC THERAPY

In order to understand the important mystery of the incarnation—not that of Jesus Christ but that of you yourself—the old problem of the mind-body relationship must be revived in an existential context. The problem cannot be handled here exhaustively by any means, but a few

* Some of the examples in this chapter are derived indirectly from workshops which Stanley Keleman and I conducted together at Esalen.

specific comments about the practical applications of these philosophic insights can be made.

The first key point is a reference to themes A 2 and C 3 of the master table. Required for a discussion of the fact that you are your body is a clear understanding of two basic phenomena: (1) "consciousness" refers to the here-pole, the ego zone (the transcendental region) of the continuous stream of experience that is the phenomenon of life and (2) "body" or "world" refer to the object zone, the there-area (the empirical or psychological region) of that polarized field.

The second point needed to explain the phenomenon of embodiment is that one aspect of understanding anything requires a stirring up of reality (the world, the body, the objective area) so that it will divulge all its contents and present to the eye all that which is hidden in its sedimentation. An emotional or physical trauma stirs up the sedimented layers of a person's life and exposes them for viewing. This point makes sense because of the existential position that feelings and emotions are part of the objective world (the empirical ego, the body-as-mine) and not part of the subjective consciousness which I am. Understanding presupposes data and information. We must find ways to make the world show us its contents.

Here is where psychotherapy comes in. What shakes up most, what— like an earthquake—rattles most effectively the personality or the empirical ego are the phenomena of transference and countertransference. These are terms borrowed from psychoanalysis. When patient and therapist—in individual or group work—feel that what goes on between them is actual empirical reality, deep emotions will be stirred up. When real feelings develop between patient and therapist, the emotional atmosphere—the intersubjective field of consciousness that has been developed—will be charged with tension and become replete with energy. Everyone present in this therapeutic context must now tread very cautiously—such tension has explosive as well as curative potentials.

The individuals in a state of transference or countertransference can feel themselves ignored, rejected, destroyed, seduced, kicked, attracted, provoked, overwhelmed, attacked, loved, recognized, appreciated—or experience any other of a large number of interpersonal emotional possibilities. But it is far from enough to stir up material in order to create a complete therapeutic situation.

Thus, the third point is the unequivocal need for constant distance between therapist and patient, the depth of transference and countertransference emotions notwithstanding. Only with the addition of this distance and with its expert management does the situation become authentically therapeutic. The distance is achieved by asking and responding to questions such as "What is happening here?" "What part of me is being disclosed?" "What pattern am I repeating?" "Why am I resisting?" The technical phenomenological name for this distance is *epoche,* or *reduction,* and it is central to the existence of any cognitive situation.

It then follows that a bona fide therapeutic transaction is one in which the patient-therapist relation is *always permanently* placed at a psychic distance, "reduced" or put in an epoche. The epoche must be maintained *at the same time that the relationship (the transference and countertransference) is intensified and deepened.* That intensification is the pain but it is also the learning experience. This process is emotionally thoroughly exhausting.

Maintaining intense transference and countertransference phenomena at an intellectual distance (an epoche or a transcendental reduction) has two results. First, it leads to great insight about the nature of one's empirical ego or psychological ego, his bodily and emotional being-in-the-world. That is gain enough. Secondly, it gives access to the pure subjective consciousness (the ego pole of the field of consciousness) that we all are—access to transcendental experience. As we become more capable of resting securely in the frightful emptiness that is the consciousness of man's freedom, a transformation takes place: the emptiness is no longer seen as empty. It becomes the most solid and most concrete reality in all of being, and this leads to the emergence of the courageous and unique individual.

These three characteristics of authentic therapy must be understood before embodiment can be meaningfully explained. Let me first illustrate the material covered up to now by bringing in an example—a record of a therapist-patient relationship taken from notes, mostly those dealing with the therapist's countertransference, of a staff meeting at _____ clinic.

Epoche

> *Patient (P)—member of a group—is female, in her late twenties, attractive, braless, and provocative. In a group of twenty-five, she makes herself seductive and places herself in the position of authority, directly opposite therapist (T). She announces that at sixteen she was raped, and that the then most significant male in her life offended her, when he heard about it, by saying, "You were asking for it!"*
>
> *As the session progresses, T tries to reach her center. He uses no tricks or techniques. In effect, he says to her "I offer you real values; I offer you my center, my love, as it were. I will speak only to your center and not to your manipulative exterior."*
>
> *T is now responding to her seductive invitation. But he tries to go beyond her seductiveness and touch her genuine transcendental center. T describes P to herself, "You have been weeping all morning. You have pursed your lips tightly. Several times you tried to speak. You never did. You did preface your apparent readiness to speak with a gesture of dangerous self-exposure. You wear heavy jewelry and a thick belt, all of which covers your vulnerable front—chest and abdomen (earlier you said this was for 'protection'). When you are ready to speak, that is, to express your-*

self, you raise your arms and clasp your fingers together behind your back. And in the end you do not speak at all."

T continues, *"Your body is saying to me that self-expression, that is, being yourself, means dangerous self-exposure. You therefore hold yourself (that is, your words) back."*

Then T adds, *"This is my message to you: Real self-expression does not mean role-playing, nor does it mean sexual seduction. It does not mean a power play either. You do not know that, or if you do, you do not act on it.*

"You are vulnerable only when you play a role (like that of the receptive female which you seem to play as an automatic response to self-expression) because you may fail in this role. You place the role in the world as your surrogate. The role may be squashed by the group like an insect. The group or the leader may be more powerful than the insect. But if your self-expression is genuine—that is, an extension of your true center—then the extruded you is unassailable."

P responded very negatively to T: *"I don't understand what you said."* She also made statements such as, *"That all seems irrelevant. I resent your arrogance. You are patronizing. You treat me like a little girl. You dominate me and tell me what to do. I am not a little girl; in fact, I hate the little girl in me."*

In summary, this is what has happened:

(1) T has said, "I'm in touch with you. We are now an intersubjective field of consciousness."

(2) P responds: "No, you're not in touch with me. We're not an intersubjective field. You are making a fool of yourself."

(3) T: "It is your contempt for me that guarantees the permanence of the separation. In truth, it is a permanent separation between your center and your bodily existence."

Here we have a schizoid alienation in which the individual as a conscious center does not exist. As such, the center is not in the body. The body lives alone, isolated, more like an animal than a person.

P calls attention to T's countertransference. P hurts T. T feels deeply wounded, even though his analysis of P may be correct. That feeling of hurt is the key to the existence of a countertransference, i.e., real empirical feelings and relations. T speaks more as a lover (empirical relation) than as a therapist (transcendental relation).

T now puts his feelings of rejection in the context of an epoche. His interpretation was rejected and thereby also his transcendental overture. He realizes he has offered P something of infinite value, on which P spits. He discovers that he comes across to P (perhaps to all patients) as (a) offering or even inviting the opportunity for rejection and (b) as permitting himself to be a scapegoat. The effect of these personality characteristics in T is to place himself in the service of the patient's resistance.

Seeing all this, T reestablishes the epoche:

T orders P: "I want you to love that little girl in you! I want you to hug that little girl, hold her tight, and tell her 'I love you!'"

P responds: "I resent being told what to do."

T's reaction: "Then I have nothing more to offer you. You are wasting my time and your money being here!"

T has now responded to P's schizoid alienation: the total refusal of P to be her center, to respond from that center, and to be touched at that center.

Several hours later P has a fantasy: "I am a happy little girl perched on a branch in an apple tree."

That is an oblique recognition that she can love the girl within her.

At a much later time, P and T came to the following conclusion. P's pattern was to seductively provoke and then to deny, a situation that invites rape. She wanted to rape her body (or have it done to her). Her center is dead and it is her body that is killing it. She has to destroy her body (which incidentally she, having large breasts, does by not wearing a bra) to liberate her center. She invites rape because she wants rape: she conspires with the rapist to destroy her body, she is raping herself. Her body is the obstruction to her conscious center. Once she has destroyed her body, that is, achieved the psychological equivalent of its destruction, she finally will have reached and saved her center. It is a case of "rape yourself or remain schizoid."

P hates T. T allows the hatred, which is mostly indifference and exclusion, to surface.

Then T comes back and asks P: "You know who I am?"

P: "No, who are you?"

T: "I am you; I am your center; I am the little girl in you!"

After a very long and tense pause, P breaks into profound, extended, and uncontrollable sobs. She has contacted her center. T puts his arms around P and reassuringly waits until P's emotions settle themselves into a new and unaccustomed organization.

P's center has been reached. T has touched P's center, and with that P has accepted her own center. T feels warmly relieved in that the reality of his own conscious center has been validated by the newly established intersubjective relation. Unfortunately, such positive results are not always forthcoming.

The above shows the importance of distance (epoche) and the kinship between distancing and mental health. The analysis also shows how violently difficult and risky it is to deal therapeutically with cases of this sort. But once body and psyche (i.e., empirical ego) have been shaken up, the consciousness (the transcendental ego) can witness the shaking body and trembling psyche finding a new place in which to organize themselves. The new organization feels natural, and it *is* natural in the sense that the decision of the consciousness is to remain an observer of the independent life of the body and of the emotions. The observer or witness posture, which can be achieved only through the act of psychic distancing (an epoche), is essential for the development of a natural, rather than forced or artificial, reorganization of the body. Here "natural" means accepting the structure of the world and choosing *not* to impose the structure of consciousness upon it.

EMBODIMENT

Passive Embodiment

Embodiment can occur either passively or actively. In passive embodiment you *observe* your body. You do not feel that you actively *are* your body but you perceive its movements, postures, and emotions. Above all, you observe your sexual feelings. You let these feelings be and allow them to run their own course. You do not direct them, you do not deny them, you do not repress them. You do not artificially seek them out, or stimulate them, nor do you interpret them. You just look at them. You are aware of them. The observer or witness status also demands that you become aware of the *absence* of sexual feelings, of the *denial* of them, and of the *deflection* or *displacement* of them. But you do not interfere. Finally, you also observe their metamorphosis into symbolic bodily or emotional sensations.

This condition of awareness without participation can be best understood in terms of the analysis of therapy presented above, because what is demanded is that sexual feelings be in a permanent epoche. Observation does not delimit or truncate sexual feelings; detached observing of the motions of one's feelings in no way restricts the course these feelings run. A peaceful rainbow over a waterfall does not stop the cascading torrent beneath. On the contrary, such observation often stirs up feelings and exposes what was hidden before, because much conscious energy was expended in closing off these feelings from awareness.

The final step in passive embodiment and sexualization is to ride the crest of these feelings; it is the decision to move unobtrusively with them, to gently touch them without affecting their progression, as if an angel were to touch the waves of the ocean. It is the decision not to direct the flow but to move with it.

The passive approach is by far the most effective form of embodiment. It preserves the independence and integrity of *both* the conscious subject pole *and* the material object pole of the field of experience or life. However, there is a second type of embodiment which is also useful.

Active Embodiment

Active embodiment is the deliberate decision to be the body, consciously to enter the body, willingly to take over the body. The significance and nature of this approach can best be presented by means of an illustration.

Sigrid

Sigrid went through what I call an "I am" exercise and experience. "I AM" was God's answer to Moses in response to his asking "Who are you?" of the bush that burned without consuming itself. Presently we shall examine Sigrid's "I am" experience step by step.

Pure consciousness, or the transcendental ego, can be experienced either as individual or as intersubjective (in which case it can be called transcendental intersubjectivity).* In an emotionally charged roomful of people—as in group therapy or encounter groups—consciousness is most accurately described as an intersubjective phenomenon. In a crowd, consciousness may or may not be experienced as an individual phenomenon. To be an individual partly means to be in touch with consciousness, regardless of whether that consciousness is individual or intersubjective. In either case, the sense of individuality, reality, consciousness, centeredness (the "I am" experience) exists.

However, individualism means more than simply to feel oneself as an ascetically pure individual or intersubjective consciousness. I am a living individual, a person only to the degree that I have translated being a consciousness into *worldly* phenomena. To be an individual is to have incarnated that pure consciousness, to have made it into a being-in-the-world. And to be a being-in-the-world means to have united that pure consciousness with thoughts, feelings, emotions, my body and then to reach out to the world of people and things beyond.

In other words, if the decision for individualism is the decision to exist *in the world,* then it must be *embodied;* it must be incarnated; it must be materialized. And the key word in active embodiment is *power.* Power is the physical extrusion of the pure, conscious and silent center, of the ultimate and transcendental self, out into the substantial world of bodies and things. It is the phenomenon of resolve, resoluteness, and commitment. Power is how consciousness feels as it descends through the body, responds to the pull of gravity and the resultant rootedness and groundedness of that body. Power is the name for the movement of the body out into the world, either by walking or by voicing—since language is another fundamental expression of our being-in-the-world. (To *ex-press* is to press out —like giving birth to a baby—it is a function of bodily movement, of speech, of art.) Expression is synonymous with the self-transcending character of love. And love—like all growth—is a general connectedness with the world, a general being in the world, and not something restricted to the relationship between two people. An authentic person is not "in love"; he does not find "the right person." Rather, a person who has authentically embodied himself is permanently capable of love and relates

---

* The notion of cosmic consciousness does not concern us here in this therapeutic setting.

himself unfailingly to all aspects of life, animate and inanimate, personal and impersonal, in a loving, giving, open and intimate fashion.

Now back to Sigrid's experience. She was approached as follows:

> T (*Therapist*): "*Accept me into your being as yourself. I shall speak with your voice and for you.*
>
> "*I am your consciousness seeking embodiment. . . . I am heavy and weighty. Feel me descend in your body, from the head, through the neck to the chest and the abdomen. You feel full and heavy inside. Now allow that weight to go down to your feet. They now feel firmly implanted on the ground. They are grounded solidly, like the roots of a tree.*
>
> "*Now walk forward, with heavy and deliberate steps. Make a fist with each hand, feeling at all times your power, hold your fists before you in a gesture of resolve, open your eyes and say, from as deep as you can bring your voice, 'I am!' As you walk, meet the world with your pelvic region. Extrude your genital region, which is the bottom of the torso, the base of the seat of feelings.*"

As Sigrid was performing this exercise of incarnation she cried and trembled, alternately opening her hands in a pleading gesture and clenching her fists in a sign of resolve. She resolutely said, "I am," and immediately thereafter she stammered, "I can't, I can't!" She alternately opened and closed her eyes, moved forward, and stopped. The open eyes signified contact with the world of her embodiment. The closed eyes meant alienation. It was obvious that Sigrid wavered ambiguously between worldly self-affirmation and nonaffirmation, between hedonistic embodiment and ascetic isolation. Her inability to complete the exercise fully was evidence of her partial rather than total incarnation. It was a highly dramatic display of philosophy in action. It was a demonstration of the active being-in-the-world of a consciousness.

Embodiment becomes differentiated as sexual or as narrowly genital when its focus—the source of the outward movement—is at the base of the torso, that is, the pelvic region. Full embodiment begins in the pelvis but does not remain there: Its waves of energy radiate into the entire body.

Sigrid can enhance her embodied being-in-the-world by using this exercise for practice in living. As she becomes more adept at this exercise she will also carry over her embodiment from the consulting room to her daily life. We have here a good illustration of *active* embodiment.

The authentic individual is one in whom the field of consciousness is whole. He is an individual in whom subject and object, consciousness and body, are distinct yet truthfully connected. The absence of that connection, of that flow, is alienation, which is perhaps the most common phenomenon found in so-called healthy people. Its symptom in daily life is a sense of meaninglessness and in general a feeling of the emptiness of existence. Exercises and experiences dealing with both active and passive embodiment can help overcome this schizoid condition.

12

Existential Sex

The Sexual Partner
as Object and as Subject

If the first theme of existential sex is body authenticity, the *second* is that the sexual partner can be perceived as an object, a thing, rather than as a human subjectivity. This may appear contrary to the existential principle of reverence for subjectivity (principle C 6a of the master table), but we shall see that such is not the case.

The Partner as Object

Ideal sex should reflect the essence of man. A human being, in his philosophical essence, is *both* a subject and an object. Love is the encounter which recognizes the subjectivity of the other or the partner. But ideal sex must also allow for the full experience of the partner as mere object. We must now explore together how the sexual experience can be enhanced and deepened by focusing on the fact that the partner in sexual love is *also* an object, the objective pole of the field of consciousness that I am.

The ego-world continuum has an objective pole, as well as a subjective pole. We can now focus on the objective pole of the field of consciousness *exclusively*. The sexualization—that is to say, the symbolic incarnation—of this philosophical reality is the act of *preparing* the sexual partner for love-play and intercourse. In this case the partner is not met or encountered, but is decorated and primped like any precious thing or object.

It does not matter who plays the role of object and who the role of subject in this sexualization of human reality. In existential sex the couple decides who is the subject and who is the object in the sexual relationship, at any one particular given time. In the chapter on love the point was made that all authentic human beings—men and women alike —are *both* male *and* female (that is, both subject and object at the same time). An existential love relationship is possible only between individuals who are *whole* in this sense. As they relate, one of them will emphasize the male (subject) pole while the other will emphasize its complement, the female (object) pole. There is no preordained rule in the nature of human beings as to which individual in the relationship adopts which sexual role. In existential sex, the male and female roles are interchangeable. If the female adopts the role of subject, then her self-assigned task might be to undress her partner, to bathe or shower him, to shampoo his hair, to rub him with lotions, perhaps to judiciously use perfumes of some kind, and to massage him (although massage can also be used to establish and express subjective loving encounter).

The male as the subject and the female as the object are no more than social conventions. We are fields of consciousness first and sexual, role-playing organisms second. Paul, one of my private students, told me that he went so far as to design his wife's clothes, even underwear, and direct her body-building calisthenics. He assured me they both found this activity very pleasurable and exciting as sexual foreplay. Both of them, however, understood it to be sexual foreplay and not some kind of neurotic male chauvinism. Sandra, his wife, freely chose the role of object in one part of their sexual relationship.

Consciousness is prior to sex and that consciousness is asexual. The sexualization of consciousness is a free decision and a free construction. It is therefore healthy to place both male *and* female in the roles traditionally assigned to the male alone.

At this point you are entitled to be somewhat puzzled. On the one hand you are told that existentialism stresses our inescapable subjectivity and that ignoring subjectivity dehumanizes us all. Now, you are told to go back to the old ghost-in-a-machine theory of man in order to enjoy sex more fully. It is of course true that we are objects *in addition* to being subjects. The existential emphasis on subjectivity is in part a reaction to the cultural emphasis on materialism, mechanism, and the objectivity of man.

But how can the sex object (the female in the usual case) enjoy sex authentically? Indeed, many a woman gets neurotic satisfaction out of being a sex object. She may achieve financial security and satisfy her exhibitionist tendencies. She may also satisfy some of her masochistic needs. But how can an authentic woman find meaning in being a sex object?

Since I do not wish to be understood as saying that men and women are essentially different, it may be useful to rephrase this question as follows: How does the subject pole (male) of the field of consciousness that each human being is enjoy sex? And how does the object pole (female) of that field enjoy sex? How can sex be enjoyed by the *total* person, the subject-object combination, the male-female integration?

Bryan and Thelma

Let us take the case of Bryan and Thelma M. as illustration. Following are excerpts from some of their letters:

You were of much help to Bryan and myself before our marriage while we together were students in one of your private workshops on Wednesday evenings. After a year and a half of marriage I feel (Bryan agrees) that sex is getting stale. Our main attraction to each other was sexual and it has been the beautiful sex we have together that made our life good. Frankly, we want to keep it that way.

However, lately intercourse has become a duty and a chore rather than the glow of joy it was only a short year ago, especially the way it was on our honeymoon on lovely Vancouver Island. . . .

We enrolled in your workshop again to work out this issue (it isn't really a problem, yet). For the time being we prefer that you discuss it anonymously.

I knew Bryan and Thelma to be authentic people and as deeply and sensitively devoted to each other as any two people I could think of.

I suspected something had changed in their role-playing, and that they might discover it if they could seriously pursue a simple fantasy exercise. My suggestion was that both of them try to recapture at least in imagination the exact feeling of sexual satisfaction they had during their honeymoon. Before long, I received the following interesting communication, this time from Bryan, to be discussed anonymously in the workshop.

Your simple suggestion had amazing results. I did not believe it would. It was also a pleasure to go through the exercise.

At first, Thelma and I did not think it worth the bother. But we started reminiscing. I used to undress Thelma and bathe her and wash her hair. She also posed for me. I found that very exciting and she did also. She was passive and loved it. On our honeymoon she wanted to play the role of pin-up girl for me. Now, however, she resents me when I tell her I enjoy treating her like a sex-thing. She says that's sub-human. And I feel guilty. On our honeymoon she was the willing object in the sexual foreplay, as you said. But recently she no longer likes that at all and I just couldn't understand why. But Thelma has an answer and wants to state it in her own words.

Bryan

The letter continues in Thelma's handwriting,

I asked myself, what changed? Why do I resent now what I formerly loved? How am I different today from the Thelma of a year ago? I really don't think Bryan has changed. Your philosophy has the answer for me.

I was able to get pleasure out of the object role but I no longer can. That is

*the root of our sexual problem. And I have been racking my brain to figure out
why I once liked the object role but don't now. It shouldn't really matter, should
it, except that I feel that I have the obligation to make Bryan happy.*

*I think back to the delights of our honeymoon! I loved Bryan then. I am
afraid I love him less now. That's the difference. On our honeymoon I identified with Bryan. I really did. It's amazing to me now to realize how much I
identified with him. In fact, I was him, I believe! Making me the object gave
him pleasure and excitement and I found pleasure and excitement in it because
I was one with him! In your language, Dr. Koestenbaum, Bryan was the subject
and my body was the object in our relationship—but my soul was one with his
soul. My consciousness was the subject in your field-of-consciousness theory of
man idea. My consciousness was in the same place as Bryan's consciousness. And
my body was the object to my own consciousness, just as it was for Bryan. Thinking back I feel that we must have had the sweetest sex on earth! Perhaps only a
woman deeply in love can split herself up this way.*

*I now feel more distant from Bryan than during our honeymoon. I look out
for myself and I am not willing to identify with him or to see things through his
eyes alone. I guess I am no longer as loving and devoted as I was then. Since I
don't identify with him, I cannot experience the subject aspect of sexual love . . .
as long as I'm the object.*

*Neither of us, Dr. Koestenbaum, should think of this as tragic. The insight
of our growing independence has been beautiful. Maybe we should be satisfied
with that. Maybe I should be more aggressive, be the subject myself!*

*I know you will suggest to us that we make the decision to play again the game
we played on our honeymoon. If I choose to fully sexualize my life again (I am
not choosing that now) I think I can recapture our honeymoon bliss. I have
enjoyed being the sex object by being Bryan and I know I can make that decision
again. I'm not sure which way I will go. I am today choosing my independence.*

Love,
Thelma

In other words, a full sexual experience includes making the partner
into an object. In turn, that experience consists of the object-partner
(Thelma in this case) making the decision to identify herself fully with
the subjective consciousness of her partner. And that is an ultimate act
of love and devotion. But if there is no deep love then there can be no
such trusting transfer of consciousness. This point demands considerable
study and serious reflection; its importance is easily underrated.

We have spent enough time on the sexual object. Let us now turn to
the perception of the partner as *subject* in existential sex. You should
now review the characteristics of existential love discussed earlier in
Chapters 2–5 (which are also summarized in the questionnaire on existential love at the end of Chapter 5). We are then ready to show how these
philosophical characteristics of human encounter can be translated into
a physical sexual experience, how love can be embodied.

THE EMBRACE IS THE UNIVERSE

The sexual embrace can become the total universe and its complete history. That is the *third* theme of existential sex. Existential sex is the incarnation of a cosmic truth and an eternal reality. The sexual partners must therefore make a double decision: (1) to exclude everything but each other from consciousness and (2) to expand their touching bodies to encompass all of being and all of reality. Their embrace follows the directives of a yoga exercise: "Focus on a small aspect of your environment, like a point; exclude all else from your consciousness; be aware only of this point. Now expand this point so that it becomes infinitely large, so that nothing exists outside of that point." In this fashion the sexual embrace is made cosmic.

How, from a practical point of view, can these sexual goals be achieved? The physical environment must suit the need. The couple must be in a location that is free of interruptions and distractions. The mere thought that a phone might ring or that someone might knock on the door is an excessive distraction for existential sex. The ideal place for making love is complete isolation, for existential sex is, after all, a meditation exercise. In addition, semidarkness is necessary, because light calls attention to that part of the world which is to be eliminated from consciousness. Light can successfully be cast on each other's bodies on order to illuminate the embodiment of all reality, but since the world is now limited to two bodies, all else must be darkened into nothingness.

Physical health is required. Existential love-making is an act of creation, it is an aesthetic construction or constitution; it is the reconstruction of the world—the destruction of one and the creation of another. And reconstitution requires physical energy. But since the universe becomes the body, the life of the universe can be expressed only in the life of an energetic and healthy body. Similarly, distractions arising from the pressure of time ("We have only one hour," "It's getting late") and from feelings of guilt ("We're not married," "It was only last week that I slept with someone else," etc.) must be eliminated if authentic sex is to be achieved.

The psychological suggestions for achieving the cosmic embrace in sex are like meditation exercises. The existential lovers must practice the art of concentration. Some oriental love practices associated with the Mahasuka doctrine of religious sexuality are helpful in identifying sex with the totality of the universe. First, the partners decide on some focal point that is to symbolize the universe, some specific touch, kiss, caress, or way of copulation. Their connection can involve any or several of their senses: touch, sight, taste, smell. Second, the focal point of their connection must be experienced as *passive* rather than *active*. If their focal point is a caress, then both must concentrate on the feeling and not on the doing. What matters is that they each be fully conscious of how their senses feel. It is one thing simply to *use* one's hand to touch and it is quite another to be conscious of how the hand feels when it is touching. If, for example, the male gently massages the female's back, then *both* must concentrate on what they are feeling at this moment: The woman must concentrate on the sensation of being stroked and the man must concentrate on how it feels to rub gently. He must become conscious of how his hands and his fingertips feel. If, on the other hand, the woman kisses the man's ear, she must not concentrate on the *act* of kissing but on the *feel* of her own lips as she kisses. If the couple simply "looks" at each other, the focus is not on what each sees but on how it feels to do this kind of sensuous looking. Or, the couple might simply sit, facing one another, with their genitals copulating, and be passive spectators to the feelings that thus grow up independently and uncontrolled inside them.

By following these procedures—or imaginative and creative individual adaptations of them—the physical sexual sensations can be so immense that they fill the lovers' universe. The emphasis is on passivity because we become aware of the universe in being passive to it. We observe it; we perceive the world and the stars; we open ourselves up to their messages; we permit their natures to disclose themselves to us. To know is to be passive. To appreciate is to be passive. To perceive is to be the passive observer.

Now that the sexual embrace has become the universe we must turn to another philosophical aspect of the world which can be expressed in the act of love: "intentionality."

SEX IS THE STREAM OF CONSCIOUSNESS AND LIFE

The previous section was concerned with passion or passivity. This one is active. We are now turning to the *fourth* theme of existential sex. To be human is to emerge vitally with the power of a geyser from one's inmost center into the world waiting without. Here is the fundamental project of self-transcendence that is man, the essence of human consciousness itself. Herein is compressed the absolute and irreducible philosophic truth about the world. Emerging self-transcendence is the movement from the nothingness of consciousness to fullness of being. In Chapter 5 I discussed the fact that love is natural. We must now integrate that into the physical sexual experience.

In describing the field-of-consciousness theory of man, we can use the metaphors of the sunburst and the explosion. That aspect of the core structure of human existence is magnificently repeated in the conquest of sexual intercourse. The forward-thrusting penis of one human being entering the receptive vagina of another human being—underscored and intensified by the ejaculation of seminal fluid—is beyond question the best biological replica of the field-of-consciousness theory of man, of the unique dialectical relation of consciousness to the world. The field of consciousness from inside to outside is the philosophical truth about man. That one universal truth can be most obviously incarnated and made real in a physiological metaphor by the act of loving intercourse. Because of this felicitous connection between philosophy and reproduction it is possible to make sex into a religious experience.

The abstract truth never satisfies. Man needs to translate the dry philosophical reality into living experiences. That is done through myth and religion, and can be accomplished through the solid and multidimensional metaphor of the lived and living body. Sex is not the only way that the body is used to express and live a cosmic truth. Eating is made into a metaphoric ritual. Physiologically, eating is no more than ingestion of food for survival. It is instructive to see snakes and lizards eat, as well as lions and giraffes, to get an idea of how food can be consumed for survival and nutrition alone.

We are then startled when we compare this animal eating behavior with our sophisticated, ritualistic cooking and serving techniques. We cook with wine and sauté in butter; we serve with waiters and candles; we balance the textures of the foods and are fastidious about temperatures (plates for strawberries must be chilled; coffee must be piping hot, water should be cold). Dining becomes a ceremonial occasion. We celebrate birthdays, friendships, awards, and honors with meals and banquets. Fantastic sums of money are spent in adorning the simple alimentary function of eating. Eating, the symbolic ingestion of the world, is a basic biological function on which we superimpose a fantastic mythical edifice and through which we live ultimate philosophical truth and reality.

The same is true of the manner in which we dress. Dressing (and undressing) the body is another of our vastly elaborated necessities. A simple skin or robe will suffice to protect and warm the body. But in dressing we are creating a personality for ourselves and relating ourselves to the world around us. That is why undressing—as in nude encounter group marathons and in Esalen massage—readily becomes the symbol for shedding roles, defenses, and artificial values.

SEXUAL INTERCOURSE

The same symbolic value can be found in the truth of sexual intercourse. In existential sex, the body is no longer used to express relatively minor *social* relations, reproductive functions or psychological needs, but it now becomes the full being and the total history of the universe. In existential sex, the body is used to live out, metaphorically, the project, the destiny, goal, or nature of the universe and it thus becomes the meaning of life.

If sex is the metaphor for the field that extends from ego to world, then sex cannot be merely an experience restricted to one organ or one region of the body. It has to be felt as an expression or impression of the total person—body and soul. The authentic sexual experience begins in the pelvis and expands in overwhelming waves throughout the full body. The orgasm is then a total bodily discharge, a transcending movement beyond the self, not just a genital function and experience. The orgasm is thus not a genital phenomenon at all; it is a body-phenomenon or a person-phenomenon. In the last analysis, it is a cosmic phenomenon akin to the creation of the world.

How can a couple accomplish the fullness of this cosmic metaphor? Three obvious suggestions come to mind. First, the couple must possess an understanding of the philosophical or existential nature of man. They must be reasonably sophisticated in their familiarity with these ideas. That task is one of the goals of the present book. It is also developed in my book *Managing Anxiety* (Englewood Cliffs, N.J.: Prentice-Hall). Second, the couple must have ample experience integrating these philosophic ideas into their general nonsexual life. In short, they must be mature, self-actualizing, and well-adjusted persons. They must be authentic. Third, they must possess a poetic nature. They must be endowed with the capacity to appreciate metaphor and to live in and through symbols. The study of poetic symbolism, as well as a living familiarity with other art forms, is a distinct asset in the sexualization of human existence. The couple is expected to understand the metaphoric possibilities of sexual intercourse. Only to the extent that they have a developed sense of the arts, which exhibit the most beautiful and efficient use of metaphor, are they capable of existential sex.

The roles of the male and the female are different from each other when sexual intercourse is used as the metaphor for self-transcendence. The sexual relation is a vector: it has a direction, a thrust, a here and a there, a subject and an object. The common prejudice that it is "natural" for the male to be aggressive and conquering and for the female to be passive and submissive has its roots in the confusion between the field of consciousness and the body. If we believe that a human being is the body and that sex is the body's central function, then the domination of the male follows from the mechanics of copulation. If, on the other hand, we recognize the primacy of consciousness over man's physiological nature, then we discover that the *meaning* of copulation is the free decision of two independent human agents. Once a couple has become liberated in this philosophical sense, they can choose freely their place in the metaphor of copulation.

From the point of view of a materialistic ghost-in-a-machine theory of man, the penis is always the aggressive agent and the vagina, the passive recipient. This interpretation follows from the ghost-in-a-machine premise that a human being *is* his penis or her vagina (i.e., the body). In reality, a human being is a free consciousness; activity and passivity are free role choices. The meaning of sexual activity is not preordained by human anatomy but is created by the free choices of liberated men and women.

BACK TO BRYAN AND THELMA

Let us now examine how the cosmic character of coitus enhances sexual experiences in practice by referring once more to Bryan and Thelma. Their family backgrounds were what could be called "traditional." The role of the male was out of the home, earning a living. He directed the family. He initiated sexual love-play and taught the female how to respond. During the early part of their young marriage, Bryan was the subject and Thelma the object in sex. Bryan decided when and how to have sex. Thelma was always responsive. If he chose long foreplay, she adapted to it. If he chose immediate intercourse, she adapted to that. Thelma was always ready. She had an orgasm whenever he was about to have one. In one of her earlier notes she had written:

I am very adaptable sexually . . . and I enjoy it. If Bryan wants to kiss and pet, and nothing else, I can go on like that all day or all night. At other times Bryan wakes me up in the middle of the night and before I know it he is in me ejaculating. I can have an orgasm immediately in the middle of the night, if he wants to. I can wait through twenty-four hours of stimulation and have no orgasm at all, if Bryan wants it.

She never took the initiative, but found herself comfortable in that servile role. However, as her later letter indicated, she was fully aware of her own fundamental urge toward transcendence. She was no different from Bryan. She chose to *be him* in the early stages of her marriage. Now she chooses to be herself. And in the end she will want Bryan to choose to be her, as she had done the year before.

The eventual discussion went something like this (these are excerpts of their dialogue from my tape):

THELMA: I'm not sure I want to be passive in sex any longer, Bryan.

BRYAN: I understand that both of us grew up programmed to take our proper role and place in bed: I decide and you follow; I'm the subject and you are the object.

THELMA: I could not enjoy the role of being a sexually dominant female. I feel more comfortable as "all woman."

BRYAN: The same is true of me. I prefer to play the game with me as the aggressor, but I certainly can learn to play the other side as well. It is as if in chess I had always played white, which moves first. I also can play black.

THELMA: I feel we have reached a deeper understanding. I feel joined to you and in touch with you not as two bodies but as two conscious centers.

BRYAN: Let us then *choose* to play the game of sex like a game of chess. I'm used to white and you're used to black. Let us decide to take these positions and enjoy the game and not the positions. Perhaps at another time we can reverse colors and enjoy the game just the same.

THELMA: O.K. I play black—the object—if you play white—the subject. When I feel that I *choose* my role as sex object, then I can identify with you in orgasm. I feel *you* choose to be the subject in our relationship but that you would, if I wanted you to, play the role of object as well.

I feel closer to you, spiritually and not in terms of hormones, than ever before, Bryan. (Both weep, then hug.)

Thelma then added the following in a note she handed me later:

I am no longer the object alone in the subject-object self-transcendence. Bryan is no longer the subject alone in the philosophical project of self-transcendence. I identify with him. I am *the receiving object and I* become *the thrusting subject, so that I am all of being. Bryan* is *the emerging subject and becomes* also *the receiving object. We fully identify with each other and experience much more mature sex in this fashion.*

As we have seen, certain physical phenomena literally illustrate self-transcendence. Just as the penis juts out into the world in true self-transcending fashion, so do the breasts jut out—reaching from the ego to the world beyond. And just as the sexually excited penis ejaculates into the world, so does the stimulated breast of the post-partum female express itself by "expressing" milk to the receptive and needing other, the infant.

Breast-feeding in the female has the same symbolic role as ejaculation for the male. In both, the inside literally moves out into a receiving world. And, conversely, that ejaculation in intercourse has the same symbolic meaning for the female—she is placed in a passive-receptive position—as being fed has for the male—in which the female symbolically feeds milk to the receptive male.

It follows that the complete existential sexual experience involves (1) intercourse and ejaculation, (2) the female's awareness of the seminal fluid, (3) having children, (4) breast-feeding these children and (5) the female feeding the family, including the male partner.

SEXUAL SURRENDER

The sexual experience in its existential fullness is the extraordinary experience in which an isolated and alone subjectivity is given the free gift of another soul. This theme is the *fifth* in the exposition of existential sex. It is crucial that this gift, this act of grace, be clearly visualized. Let us say for purpose of illustration that the woman gives herself to the man, although the reverse would of course be equally possible. At least eight characteristics of that act of erotic surrender can be outlined. Remember that the act of surrender is expressed in existential sex through the giving of the body, where "giving" is done with artful movement, gesture, responsiveness, and delicate muscular balance.

1. She gives him something that he can never have or acquire on his own. He cannot *take* a woman's being, because what he wants is her willingness and her freedom. In criminal assault, or rape, the criminal may achieve intercourse but he does not receive the soul of his victim as a gift. Neither heaven nor hell can give a man the love of a woman; only a woman can do that. She does it herself, with her own freedom and out of her own volition. A man can acquire wealth and power, even slaves, but he cannot possess through his own initiative the spirit of a woman. The gift of herself is thus a gift that only a woman can offer to a man. And the gift has to be of herself—not of another.

2. The gift is truly an act of grace, since the gift is undeserved. To receive a totally undeserved gift from one who gains nothing from it and has no need to give it is an ineffable and unique experience. Only the language of religion has been able to express adequately the devastating and euphorically elevating effect the grace of an undeserved gift has on the human consciousness. To receive the gift of love is the experience of conversion. It feels as if the pulsating stream of life had been infused into what was until then a corpse.

3. The gift in surrender is of infinite value. Perhaps the woman's personality is not worth much; perhaps her body's health is waning. The empirical ego of any person is not of infinite value. Some empirical egos are more valuable than others. What is of infinite value, however, is the transcendental ego behind the empirical ego. This point evolves from principle A 2 of the master table ("I am a pure consciousness that has a psychological personality, a physical body and many social roles"). And that pure inward consciousness of every human subjectivity is of infinite worth. As principle C 6a states it, "Each individual human inward subjectivity is the divine consciousness in man." That center is also a freedom, as seen by principle C 7 ("I always choose because I am always free"). In surrender, that center makes a gift of itself to another. It makes the ultimate sacrifice of itself, since it gives what is the most valuable of all there is, anywhere in the universe.

4. There is no need or reason to give the gift. The giving is an act of the purest freedom. A woman gives herself to the man she chooses to love (and vice-versa) in an act of pure spontaneity, in a creation out of nothing. The woman who gives her inward consciousness in love does it with

sheer self-determination. She expects no rewards and she sets no conditions.

5. The male experiences a conflict. To deserve this monumental gift of another freedom he must be perfect, like God himself: He must be his transcendental ego. But in actual fact his emphasis has been mostly on his empirical ego and he is therefore overwhelmed by the power and the beauty of this gift of love. His glowing bliss is also the conflict of emphasis between these two egos within him. What is he to do with an undeserved gift? How is he to respond when infinite God gives himself to his finite and worthless self? This kind of love is experienced by the male as the deep tragedy of contradiction. He must be God but he is only man. Existential surrender is sweet tragedy; it is dulcet pain. This point is made in principle C 14 of the master table. ("The inescapable ambiguities and contradictions of life are my powerful allies").

6. The male alone is incomplete. The experience of authentic intimacy, which is a "dialectical" experience, is unique. To reduce it to terms already known is to be insensitive to the warming glory of the experience of surrender. A happy and successful man cannot understand the joys of sexual surrender in terms of his bachelor happiness. Bachelor happiness is incompleteness. The sweet love experienced in mutual conquest and mutual surrender is an experience of dialectical, interacting, and responsive completeness. He is now two instead of one. He has now acquired his complement. In the gift of a freedom's surrender, fragmented man is reborn and recreated as a new whole, a being in whom all parts are present and fit together.

7. The reasons for the power and significance of the conquest-surrender relationship is that in it the *unity in duality* which is the essence of the human loving encounter is most clearly expressed. Conquest means that one has become two without losing the individual difference of either. Similarly, surrender means that one has become two without vanishing. The woman does not evaporate into nothingness when she surrenders. On the contrary, she retains her integrity. The male does not destroy the female when he conquers; if he did, the conquest would not be worth having. The conquest is desirable because it yields an independent consciousness. In conquest and surrender we find a true unity of duality.

The conquest-surrender relationship is the profound experience that existential sex can be because it embodies the *dialectical* character of human nature. Love is thus akin in depth to tragedy in art. The ability to embrace tightly while retaining individuality is the heart of the dialectic of all being. Existential sex gives full expression to that aspect of personal and cosmic reality.

8. Sadism is clearly not a part of an authentic existential sexual encounter. The sexual pleasure for the sadist lies precisely in the surrender of the freedom of his victim. When his victim cries "I surrender of my

own free will"—when the victim says, in effect, "You have reached my center, you have touched my conscious core; I understand that I am completely and irrevocably in your possession"—then the sadist's pleasure is at its peak. But the extraordinary difference between sadism and authenticity is again as ignorance is to knowledge. The sadist's personality structure does not "know," as it were, that the freedom which results from coercion or deceit is no freedom at all. The sadist is still a child: He thinks he can get his way by imposing his will on others through force. He inflicts punishment to achieve his way or he affects a puerile temper tantrum. In fact, the sadist experiences the failure of his force. He may even kill his victim in despair at the discovery that it is a contradiction in terms to force the surrender of one's freedom. God cannot be forced to create the universe; a woman cannot be forced to surrender her being.

The mechanics of conquest and surrender, to be made real, are translated in existential sex into bodily phenomena. To translate a philosophical reality into the flesh of two embracing human beings is one of the greatest art forms of mankind. It is an art form for which the predisposition may be innate, but the nuances and the development are not. The art of love, that is, the translation of a transcendental meeting of two consciousnesses into bodily actions and reactions, is learned like the playing of a violin to perfection. It is an art like a consummately accomplished dance. The art of love requires a lifetime of devotion; it demands that love be the full meaning of the artist's life.

Surrender is the most delicate expression of femininity. Surrender makes it possible for a female to feel feminine and for a male to feel masculine.

PERMISSIVENESS

The conquest-surrender syndrome is most intense in the *least* permissive societies. The less that is permitted, the more there is to reveal and thus to surrender. In a *completely* free and permissive society, the possibility for sexual surrender is *totally* eliminated. Where between these two extremes do we find ourselves with our social mores today? Each person owes it to himself to answer that question fully and honestly. And that is the *sixth* theme in the discussion of existential sex.

Common forms of physical surrender are coquettish behavior, suggestive clothes, undressing and nudity, intercourse and orgasm. In varying degrees, these experiences are "rationed" and "reserved." They are "held back" for the special person or the special offering or purpose.

A society that encourages bra burning, nudity, easy sex, and pornography leads to the following consequences: Sex becomes secondary and minor. Sex is relegated to its basically biological function. Sex is removed from your life as a thorn is removed from your finger. Life can now go on without an obsession with sex. Sex is now a mere need. The aesthetic, metaphysical, religious, and philosophical possibilities that can give sex infinite meaning have been dissipated in the permissive society.

These are indeed important consequences. The downgrading of sex has advantages that are as great as are its obvious disadvantages. Our society vastly overstresses sex and thereby enslaves the population with sex. Sexual stimulation sells cars and cigarettes, the emphasis on sex breaks up marriages and produces violence and crime. Improperly managed sexual impulses interfere with learning at school and productivity at work. Indulgence in sex gets some into debt and sends others to hospitals. But on the opposite side of our ledger, we see that permissiveness destroys the possibility of experiencing the phenomenon of surrender in the flesh of one's own body and in the body of a beloved.

Surrender is the secret ingredient in the magic of first love. Surrender can be expressed with a look or in a gesture, maybe in deliberately accidental closeness. Even touching is not necessary for surrender. In fact, what makes sex sexy is not the actual physical stimulation and the response of the nervous system but the fact that a particular sexual act (from a coquettish gesture to a Reichian orgasm) expresses through human flesh the philosophical conquest-surrender syndrome. Here we have a formula and a prescription for the infinite enhancement of sexual pleasure. But as permissiveness increases, the possibilities for surrender metaphors and the extended use of them decreases sharply. A woman may at one time have aroused a man by wearing an old-fashioned one-piece bathing suit. But a society which was being desensitized in general to the metaphors of surrender soon required the bikini to achieve arousal. This process of the permissive society has no end, moving on to the monokini, which is the last citadel of suggestiveness.

Another issue that can be discussed at this point is the question of sex before marriage. From the point of view of the ontological metaphor of surrender, intercourse should be saved for marriage. Marriage is a commitment involving surrender in a religious, social, and legal setting. The meaning of intercourse as the biological metaphor for the act of surrender thus becomes vastly enhanced.

I am not suggesting here that a strict Victorian moral code be adopted. A strictly conservative moral code in sexual matters—in addition to the sexual maladjustments (such as conversion hysteria) to which it gives rise —presupposes also that sex is the most important aspect of life. Sexual conservatism assumes that the sexualization of life is the meaning of life (which makes Freud a conservative!). But it is a central contention of the existential way of life and love that the role of sex in life is chosen freely by each individual. That role is not to be set by society or by science. The meaning of the sexual experience and its relative importance in one's life are purely individual matters. They are the private province of every citizen and cannot be invaded by custom, religion, law, or by any expert, neither medical nor psychological. But let us not forget that in a permissive society, sex is of secondary importance.

The orgasm is the ultimate possible expression of surrender. This point, in this context, speaks out against the value of masturbation. In a person who is frigid or impotent, the whole mechanism of surrender is not working. More precisely, the conquest-surrender syndrome in the individual's being-in-the-world is not functioning. The cure for that condition is then to be found by addressing ourselves to the general mode of being-in-the-world which refuses either to surrender or to conquer. The refusal is a choice and not a *fait accompli*. In other words, impotence and frigidity are malfunctions in the field of consciousness of the individual in question. That malfunction is chosen and over it the individual must assume full responsibility. The cure lies in a change of lifestyle and in philosophical maturity and not in novel physiological manipulations of sex organs. In fact, empirical research shows that *neither* practice *nor* the elaborate techniques discussed in marriage manuals can increase sexual responsiveness.*

* Seymour Fisher, *The Female Orgasm: Psychology, Physiology, Fantasy* (New York: Basic Books, 1972).

13
Existential Sex
The Beautiful

The criteria for sexual beauty form the *seventh* theme of existential sex. Of course, these criteria vary from culture to culture and from epoch to epoch. That sex can be beautiful remains, nevertheless, a u..versal truth. We must isolate the nature of that truth so that we can apply it to current sexual situations. If we know what makes sex beautiful we can also enhance its beauty in the lives of all people: This matter is particularly relevant in relation to recent efforts to assist the disabled in achieving sexual gratification. This goal can be accomplished by training healthy tissue—other than the usual erogenous zones—to become erogenous.

What will help us most in understanding the nature of sexual beauty is the section of Chapter 2 dealing with the resistance in existential love. Beauty in sex is experienced when resistance to the self-transcending advances of one ego are met with the optimum amount of resistance from the ego of the other, the love object—optimum resistance is, in fact, artful surrender.

Artful resistance to possession is the key to sexual beauty. *Sexual beauty* is present in all human beings, not those alone whose bodies are socially judged to be "beautiful." As a result of this analysis we can also begin to deal with the very serious problem faced by "ugly"—that is, deformed, unattractive, and disabled—people.

Our culture underscores the importance of *youthful* bodily beauty as

100

a precondition for beauty in sex. The men and women that our magazines, movies, and television hold up before their passive and willing audiences as models of sexual beauty are all within a narrow age bracket and conform to a narrow range of measurable physical specifications. This procedure, a form of worship expressed by the expenditure of millions of dollars, leaves out the majority of the population. And those people of great physical "beauty" are forced to live out the neurotic fantasies of the population. But left out more than the rest are the old, the sick, and the crippled. They also need sex; and they deserve sex with beauty. But who talks about the universal right to sexual beauty, about sex for the paraplegic, for the hunchback? And for the insane?

SEX IN LATER LIFE

The person who wants beauty in sex and who does not conform to the popular standards of beauty can be helped by recognizing two basic philosophical truths: (1) the freedom of the self and (2) the resistance of the other.

An individual is free and thus flexible in defining and redefining what in sex is important to him and what is not. Great comfort can be derived from the knowledge that most of sex's nature and meaning are the result of personal free choice, *not* external standards imposed by a heartless society and an unfeeling biology. Many old people who suffer secretly because they have lost all opportunity to look like movie stars can come to realize that their pain really stems from their uncritical acceptance of the popular standards of beauty. If they become philosophically enlightened and discover that they are free to define the meaning of sex, they will freely set their own standards. And these standards will be accessible and available to them. These standards will meet their emotional needs fully and will be based on a realistic appraisal of their physiological natures. Understanding *freedom* is the first element in the creation of sexual beauty.

The good news that they can in effect have the kind of sex they want is based on a deeper understanding of the nature of sexual beauty. Older people can discover that beauty in sex is the result of free human actions, expressions of the inwardness of human freedom, and has little, if anything, to do with the physical measurements and the chronological age of the human body.

Understanding *resistance* is the second element in the creation of sexual beauty. *Sexual beauty is artful resistance to possession. That is also a general philosophical fact about the relation of man to the world. There is no limit to the variety of ways in which that underlying philosophical reality can be expressed in the interaction of two bodies. If this philosophical insight is integrated fully into the lives of people who think they have been deprived of sexual beauty, then an emotional revolution awaits them.* Let me be specific.

We have already seen that the key to sexual beauty is the artful and perfect resistance found in the body of the other *as perceived by each one of our senses.*

What *the eyes* find beautiful in sex is just enough unavailability of the other's body to tease. Unavailability points to availability. What is in fact seen works only to suggest that there is more. It is that which we do not see but know to be there which is sexually beautiful and exciting. A woman can point to her body and its availability by suggestive clothes accompanied with suggestive poses, gestures, and movements. Sexual beauty is not enhanced by removing the suggestion and disclosing all nor by being permanently covered up. It is the constant teasing that evokes the dialectical nature of the field of consciousness itself. And that can be achieved only through imaginative and novel creativity. Nudity removes the resistance and thus the ambiguity, removing sexual beauty in turn. Nudity obscures the dialectical character of human existence.

Progressive Revelation

Sexual beauty—in all the senses—is found in movement; it is not something static. Therefore, suggestiveness can never stand still. It is the element of progressive revelation that creates an atmosphere of beautiful suggestiveness. Sexual beauty as given to the eyes exists strictly in the dimension of time and in the mode of movement. Beauty in sex is therefore living. It is not a picture or a statue, but a continuously living person, relationship, and encounter. The technique of the burlesque artist capitalizes on this.

If total visual revelation is to occur, one must go beyond the sense of sight. This is the limitation of pornography. Another sense has to be invoked, such as touch, if the dialectic of progressive revelation is to continue. The burlesque performer may eventually take off all her clothes —even perform coitus on stage—but the dialectic stops unless the spectator ceases to be just that and begins to touch and fondle (and be touched by) the performer. The end of this process is of course the orgasm, and the next question, often ignored in sex manuals, is "What then?" I will discuss that in a later section.

This philosophic insight is of the utmost importance to those who are no longer young, to those who may be contemplating plastic surgery to diminish the physical signs of aging—such as face lifts, hair transplants and breast operations—and to those who have always been seriously deformed, paralyzed, or crippled. *Sexual beauty does not depend on a youthful body.* In our culture today that is indeed an important message.

NOVELTY

Youth means *novelty*, and it is novelty that is sexy. Youth is *new* and novelty is the key to excitement. Anything new is in the process of revelation. Novelty is experienced as dialectical movement: It did not exist until recently, and it is before us now in the beautiful plenitude of its being.

We find novelty in new children, in vacations, and travel, in *new* experiences, *new* acquaintances, *new* books, etc. Youth in the body is the incarnation—the making into sexual flesh—of the general idea of novelty. Novelty is success with resistance or, more accurately, the process of overcoming that resistance. We are *aware* of what is new in ways we are not conscious of things we know already. We rarely notice an old painting in a room; but replace it with an entirely different one, and immediately we notice the change. What is new suddenly appears to and resists the senses. We look right *through* that which is old; but the new stops us.

What are the practical consequences of these insights? While a young body may not be available to an old person, what *is* available, and readily so, is the free and voluntary incarnation of novelty. An old man can experience novelty with an old woman and conversely. Furthermore, since what is sexy is the opaqueness found in the new, sexual beauty is created freely, freely organized, invented (see theme A 3 of the master table). A manual can and should be prepared to help older people into greater sexual expressiveness and satisfaction by suggesting ways to rediscover novelty in their relationship. Rule one of that manual would be to create a non-Playboy environment. Rule two is to be courageously free to experiment with the many physical possibilities now open to them. And rule three would be that the criteria of sexual beauty can be transformed by remembering that *novelty* and resistance *per se* rather than arbitrary and artificial social standards create what we experience as sexual beauty.

The discovery that novelty is the essence of sexual beauty can help all persons of all ages and in all circumstances to enhance the sexual meanings and possibilities of their lives.

Two examples make the point. Marian had suffered a traumatic cancer operation the previous year. Her left breast had been completely removed. She fell into a deep depression. Alexander, her husband, was sixty-nine and Marian sixty-eight. I suggested, in passing only, that the novelty of an extended trip might place their troubled lives in a more meaningful perspective. Three months later I received the following letter from, of all places, Moscow:

We are having loads of fun on our trip and we thought you'd be interested in how we are managing. You perhaps remember us from your workshop on philosophy and health (the one subtitled "Sex and Aging") in which we dis-cussed my double sexual problem. I was disgusted with my aging body and I was traumatized into depression by my mastectomy, on top of all that!

You suggested that we get out of the Playboy *environment. We have done that in a trip to the Soviet Union. Even though sex was not the only reason for our trip, the travels have helped us sexually. I realized the same could have been achieved back in the States by controlling and structuring our environment more carefully.*

You suggested that we minimize the visual aspects of sex and emphasize touch and movement instead. You explained to us that we could "redefine" our self-concept by manipulating the environment. You told us that the emphasis on visual beauty was cultural indoctrination. We can turn it off by removing our-selves from the environment that fosters it and designing our own.

This seemed to us at first so simple a solution as to be almost naïve. As usual, you were right. We want you to know how beautifully this has worked. The warmth and feel of our old bodies represent the world itself to each other of us. We explore each other's body by touch and by movement—and turn off all the lights!—and it is like exploring the world on our travels. We have never enjoyed sex more.

On our trip our minds have been really away from what you used to call the "Miss America" and the "Playboy theory of man and woman." We have success-fully done what you told us was the reconstruction (I think you said reconstitu-tion) of the meaning of sexuality. We have made our decision on how to define sexual beauty independently of social mores. We feel centered and wonderfully happy—after all that happened to me.

I wish we were again in your workshop. We were also trying to follow your other suggestion, and that was to redefine the meaning of visible *physical beauty. Perhaps it is* possible *for me to believe that Alexander can look at my naked body with one breast drooping like a piece of leather towards the floor and where the other was just a big scar . . . ! But at my age it's not worth the trouble. I can do without thinking of myself as physically gorgeous—I avoid movies and instead read good books. We have beautiful sex between us as it is. I wish you'd tell others how beautiful sex can be at almost seventy!*

We are surrounded with newness: England, Austria, Poland and now Russia, the land of Tolstoi and Solzhenitsyn. We talk of new things and in the evening we enjoy the courageous mutual exploration of our bodies, which fills our nights with newness. . . .

Love,
Marian

THE SENSES OF SMELL AND TOUCH

The *eighth* theme of existential sex concerns itself with further con-sequences of the identification of sexual beauty with the principle of optimum resistance. The eighth theme is the meaning of smell and touch in existential sex.

Part of our delight in perfume results from pure association and training. But why should we choose to associate the smell of flowers with the beauties of sex? Perfume calls attention to the body through an added sense, the sense of smell. And perfume evokes not only the optimum resistance of the sexual partner but even more the perfect resistance of nature herself.

Perfume is the message of spring; spring which evokes the unity of the body with nature, the continuity of the self with the world. In spring, nature is closest to man; then we can truly say the world was made for man. Spring invites you to go into the fields, to loosen, and shed your clothes, to feel the mellow touch of the sun, the cooling caresses of the breeze on your bare skin, and the embrace of water in brook, lake, or sea. That is the experience of optimum otherness, of perfect resistance, of freshness and novelty, being overcome. It is a resistance that invites you to be one with nature.

The sense of smell is important to sexual beauty; vastly more important, however, is the sense of touch. Touch and movement are related to the extent that the sense of touch becomes anaesthetized if there is no caress, no movement, no rubbing, and no massage. Touch is an experience only as long as there is ever-so-slight resistance to its penetration into the object. The man's body stops the forward movement of the woman's hand as she gently touches him. Without the resistance of his body, her hand would move on forever. Unless skin rubs against resisting skin, unless there is novelty brought about by movement, there is no sensation at all. Touch alone soon loses the sense of resistance, but the caressing touch reinvokes the sense of a resistant otherness and therefore becomes the experience of sexual beauty.

Sexual beauty in touch presupposes soft, smooth, and yielding skin and flesh. As a result some parts of the body (a woman's breasts and buttocks, for example) are more emphasized in popular sexuality than others. In Western society such parts of regions are covered by clothing—and are retained as zones of suggestivity. (Let us, for future reference, call this zone Region I.) Presumably they will be the last ones to be revealed by an increasingly liberal society. They most closely fit the criteria of optimum resistance outlined above. What I am discussing here is the philosophic equivalent of erogenous zones. I make the assumption that a zone is erogenous not because it possesses a particular set of nerve endings, but because that part of the body lends itself best as metaphor for the structure of consciousness.

Next in respect to resistance (Region II) are lips, stomach, and thighs. In those regions there is less yielding flesh, and so they are more readily uncovered in our society; however, they are still important erogenous zones of sexual beauty. These are the "come-ons," the immediate invitations for sexual activity and revelation. The remaining zones (Region III) are harder to the touch and thus least beautiful sexually, and they can therefore generally be exposed. There is less muscle and flesh, more skin and bone in these parts, which include the face, the shinbones, the head, forearms, neck, upper chest, etc.

CRITERIA OF SEXUAL BEAUTY

From these considerations we can draw the following conclusions about the nature of sexual beauty. I shall continue to use the female body as illustration, recognizing that the roles could be reversed—with slightly different results. First, that part of the body which is exposed contains no (or at least a minimal) element of resistance and novelty. There is no waiting and no price to be paid for exposure of such regions as the face, head, neck, upper chest.

Second, the regions are chosen on the basis of whether or not they offer optimum resistance to the penetrating touch of the other. Hence the unfortunate breast fetish in our society. Unless a woman feels that her breasts conform to the criteria of sexual beauty demanded by the principle of optimum resistance, she is in danger of developing feelings of inferiority (theme C 14 of the master table).

Third, an ideal aesthetic body weight arises from these reflections. "Underweight" means the entire body is harder to the touch and thus less beautiful sexually. In the overweight person much of the novelty-producing contrast between body regions is lost.

Fourth, and most important, the philosophical conception of an erogenous zone has little or nothing to do with the type of nerve endings that exist at any particular part of the body. In fact, the entire theory of the importance of so-called erogenous zones in the physiology of sexual foreplay is philosophically rather meaningless. On the contrary, what makes a zone erogenous is its philosophical significance, its aptness to reflect the metaphysical being of man, the structure of the field of consciousness. A zone is philosophically erogenous to *the extent that it corresponds to the structures of the field-of-consciousness theory of man!* Sexual beauty is possible only because the body has become the metaphor for being in general. The body has become cosmic. Philosophically, nerve endings and vibrator stimulations, experience and techniques, positions and aphrodisiacs have nothing important to do with sexual excitement and sexual beauty.

And fifth, the sense of touch itself is enhanced by moisture—either the natural fluids of the body or water, oils, or lubricants added to the sexual touch. A dry hand scrapes the skin ever so slightly, but it scrapes nevertheless. A moist hand glides over the skin. The reality of the "other" is more clearly perceived in a gliding than in a scraping touch. Gliding is *optimum* otherness or resistance. Scraping is *excessive* otherness or resistance.

Beauty in sex is not in the structure of the body but such sexual beauty is a free, loving act—a mutual yielding and resisting, a dance in which as in a chamber music concert, each movement, each pitch, each rhythm, and each gesture, is both an initiating act and a yielding response.

You must always remember that sexual beauty lies in the luminous region of man's free will and not in the dark recesses of unjust fate. Although the body can be used as poetic metaphor for our relation to existence; it need not be so: The metaphor can be altered to fit the needs of the poetry. That is how a field-of-consciousness theory of man looks at the management of sex and frees us from our society's sexual prison.

After the Orgasm, What?

Today there is much talk about the orgasm. Learned and popular books and articles discuss its importance and the many problems associated with achieving it. However, what seems to be consigned to the attic of sexology is the question of what happens *after* orgasm. Is the postorgiastic couple now on the threshold of real integration and wholeness? Or have they reached the ultimate experience, beyond which is nothing? The lack of realism in an "orgasm theory of man" is like that of the proverbial romantic love story in which boy gets girl, and the book or movie ends. In truth, life *begins* when boy gets girl. Postorgasm sex thus becomes the *ninth* and last theme in the exposition of existential sex.

The existential orgasm creates the opportunity for transition from the world of symbol, metaphor, and fantasy to the reality of daily life, in which there is a world to tend, tasks to be accomplished, and ideals to be fulfilled. For the authentic musician the existential orgasm leads to the transition from living the essence of the world *through* the symbolic flesh to the practice room and the concert stage. To the authentic plumber, it leads from a moment of universal philosophic experience to fulfilling his task on earth.

However, the sharp contrast between existential sex—in which the history of the universe is compressed into a mystical euphoric experience —and life as a finite cog in a local machine in an insignificant corner of the cosmos—which is what a person's real life amounts to—seems indeed irreconcilable.

The world of mystical and aesthetic passion is in collision with the world of practical economic and social concerns. The existential lover has restricted his world to two bodies; the authentic corporation executive or politician, laborer or teacher, engineer or pilot, lives in a vast world that he cannot even begin to fathom. The lover is passive, the man of the world is active. The lover is introverted and philosophical;

the man of the world is extroverted and practical. For the lover, the extroverted and fragmented life of business is worse than meaningless: it is fake and empty. For the active participant in the affairs of the world, the life of unmitigated sexual devotion and abandon seems vastly disproportionate and even seriously neurotic. The fulltime lover is a pauper, whereas the self-made wealthy man must forgo the luxury of love.

The issue is philosophical. The orgasm signals the end of one metaphysics and the beginning of another. The first we can call philosophical and the second, practical; the first is divine and the second, human; the first is infinite and the second, finite. What is working itself out in the postorgasm experience is the religious metaphor of *God creating Himself into man,* God choosing to be finite. To be human is for the total field of consciousness (experienced in the existential preorgasm and orgasm periods) to choose itself as finite (experienced in the existential postorgasm period). It is the philosophical and theoretical problem of evil all over again. And here I must invoke the support of themes C 1 and C 2 from the master table.

Again, if I express these thoughts through traditional religious symbolism, then the transition from an existential orgasm to the practical life is told in the biblical story of Creation. God, the infinite, chose freely to limit himself by creating finite man, who is nevertheless free since man is "created in His image." That is philosophically the same as to say that infinite transcendental consciousness (God) voluntarily limits itself (and thus becomes man, as in the story of Creation or in that of the birth of Jesus) because *the infinite freely becoming finite is a greater value than the infinite remaining infinite.* God has chosen that it is better to be human than divine. Religion has well expressed the philosophic meaning of existential postorgasm sexuality.

REMEMBER

1. Existential sex requires that the body be also treated as an object.
2. In existential sex the couple decides who is the subject and who is the object in the love relationship.
3. Consciousness is prior to sex and consciousness is asexual.
4. In existential sex, the object partner identifies with the subject partner, a commitment that presupposes the devotion of love and respect.
5. The love embrace is a cosmic metaphor.
6. We must learn to be the passive observer of the sexual feelings that arise within us.
7. Sex translates the abstract field of consciousness into a lived experience.
8. Sex is a metaphysical and religious activity.
9. The orgasm is not a genital phenomenon, but a person phenomenon; it resembles the creation of the world.

10. In sexual surrender, an undeserved gift of infinite value is tendered.
11. Permissiveness destroys the potential for sexual surrender.
12. The old, the sick, and the crippled also deserve sex with beauty.
13. Sexual beauty is found where ideal resistance is found.
14. It is good news that the meaning of sexual beauty is a matter of free choice.
15. Sexual beauty is artful resistance to possession.
16. Sexual beauty does not depend on a youthful body.
17. Novelty is what brings about sexual excitement.
18. The sense of touch is the best for creating novelty.
19. The transition from orgasm to daily life is parallel to God creating the world and then choosing to define Himself as human.

14

Is Abortion Moral?

In any analysis of the philosophical problems of love, sex, and parenthood, the question of the morality of abortion must be investigated. It is a tough question because it starkly contrasts the conflict between the freedom of the couple, or of the woman, to choose their life-style (especially the freedom of the woman to control her body) and the inviolable sanctity of consciousness and of life. Both are central principles of existential philosophy. On the master table they are themes C 7 and C 6a.

When Does Life Begin?

The philosophical answer to the ethical problem of abortion comes in three parts. First, it involves the problem of when an individual life actually begins, which is not a medical issue at all. Physiology is irrelevant in answering "when does the infant begin to exist?" Actually, the medical truth is that the answer to this question is ambiguous. It is that ambiguity which is an objective scientific fact.

For example, on one extreme, it is a demonstrable biological fact that the infant began to exist at the beginning of the world, since the atomic ingredients for his body were already in existence at that time. Or, to take a less extreme example, we can say that the potentialities for any particular infant were established when his parents decided on marriage. We can move also in the other direction and adopt the extreme position that the person is created or established only at the glorious moment of full self-disclosing self-consciousness—an event that might not occur until old age, if at all! Thus, the answer to the question "When does an individual begin to exist?" is *known* to be absolutely ambiguous. The history of living organisms is a chemical and cellular continuum—a continuum with one of its ends the beginning of the world and the other, the termination of the world. To assign one particular point in that continuum as the beginning of a new life is not a biological or a medical prerogative. From the point of view of biology, cells and organisms are not discrete objects but continuous in time, generation after generation.

The second part of the answer to the question of the ethics of abortion follows from the first: Determining when life begins is an arbitrary yet gargantuan decision. Yet the decision must be made and is made. Objects and things are created by the constitutive powers of the human mind. Objects are organizations put together by the mind. For example, we are free to call Siamese twins one or two. We are free to call a desk and its drawer one or two. We are free to think of a fish as separate from the fishbowl, and we are equally free to think of both as one ecosystem. There exist conventions on how to use words, but these are not necessarily representative of the structure of reality.

Usually decisions on how to use words do not have world-shaking consequences. However, when the decision is "Where and when does the object we call 'a new person' begin?" the consequences are staggering. We then curse the day we discovered that we are free!

Fortunately for those who succumb under the anxiety of decision making, society, through its laws and institutions, has made forced decisions about precisely when a new individual begins. One type of decision is that the child begins at the *idea* of conception; as a result any interference with fertilization through the use of contraceptives would be viewed as the destruction of a child. Others hold that conception is the beginning of the development of a fertilized egg, therefore any abortion, even during the first month, is held to be murder. A third view is that the child does not begin to exist until the fourth month, and abortion prior to that is considered moral. In the latter case, the decision has been made to call the fertilized egg and its early growth a "nonperson" and the cellular organization beyond that stage, a "person." Even though this decision is arbitrary and free, it does mobilize our deepest emotions. Finally, there is the view that the person which is the child begins to exist at birth; abortion until the eighth month or so then becomes legitimate.

FREE CHOICE

In a totally free society—one in which each individual subjectivity is paramount—each individual affected would have to make for himself the monumental decision of whether or not to abort a birth. But strictly speaking, the decision is not about abortion—whether it is wanted or not is a practical consideration and an emotional fact; the decision is about a philosophical definition, about the beginning of man. It is a question of meaning and not of fact. The source of the answer is an anguished free decision and not the secure discovery of a medical truth. Herein lies its danger and its glory. While it may be easy to decide whether or not one wants an abortion, it is a mammoth impossibility to decide—not for oneself, but for all mankind—the precise point in time at which an individual person actually begins.

The agony about abortion is in truth the agony about an individual ego being truly philosophical. The philosophy of the situation is the anguished pain, not the practical decision.

A third aspect of the abortion problem is the question of the distinction between mother and fetus. Is the fetus part of the mother, or is it an independent being? That question also has no objective answer; it is absolutely ambiguous. Since in our ghost-in-a-machine theory of man we deal in terms of bodies, the question is real to us only while the child is still in the womb. The decision for abortion then is one of choosing the boundaries of mother and child. No medical authority can *discover* the answer to that question through X-rays, autopsies, or extensive studies in physiology and research in anatomy. The answer is a decision that must be made. If the decision is that the fetus is part of the mother, then the mother has the right to choose over it, and talk about "dominion over our own bodies" is meaningful. If the fetus, however, is freely defined as independent of the mother, then the constitutional guarantees that apply to all of us apply to the fetus as well. Under these latter circumstances a woman has no jurisdiction over that part of, or in her, because the fetus is not an organ.

In other words, the third aspect of the problem of abortion is the ambiguity between organ and organism. The answer is not proffered by additional researches in biology. The answer does lie in a profound and free decision: As the host organism, "am I to define the fetus in me as an organ of my body?" In this case abortion would be the decision of the woman. Or "am I to define the fetus as an independent organism?" In this case it is *not* part of a woman's body, and it possesses the full complement of constitutional guarantees.

Fortunately for those who eschew the despair of authentic decisions and self-definitions, the political structure has taken upon itself to render these philosophical decisions for all of us through the laws of the state or the church.

15

Marcia and Bella

I shall discuss the application of an existential personality theory to marriage counseling by quoting from some correspondence I had in connection with a class for adults. The correspondence was part of the classwork.

MARCIA

I received the following succinct written appeal in one of my classes.

My marriage and my family are failures. The kids fight, are insolent and disobedient. The oldest is on pot and failing in high school. The others are doing no better. One of them shoplifts. Our sex life is atrocious. Tim and I fight all the time, and it's reflecting on the kids. The most important things to me in my life are my husband and my children. All lies in ruins. Help!

Marcia

I wrote the following letter to Marcia, both for her sake and for general class discussion (that is, to illustrate existentialist principles).

The philosophical decisions you have made and are now making about who you are and what the world is (self-concept and world-concept) are reflected in the kind of living person you are and the kind of living world that surrounds you. In other words, the person you are is the person you have defined yourself to be and the family in which you live is the family you have defined into existence.

Your letter says, in effect, the time has come to take full responsibility for your world, that is, for your empirical ego and for your Life-World (your personality and your family).

113

In my response to Marcia, I am referring to theme A 3 (responsibility) of the master table. Her letter gave me the opportunity to discuss the profound meaning of the banal little phrase, "You are responsible for your life." An adult takes lonely charge of the direction of his life and assumes full personal responsibility for all events; a child looks for excuses and protects himself from maturity through self-pity.

Our empirical realm—our body, our personality, and our social milieu —is a combination of the raw data that the world thrusts upon us, data that are both ambiguous and beyond our control, *and* of our decisions, choices, and interpretations of these raw data, which *are* under our free control. The authentic individual understands that self- and world-definitions are his responsibility, and he willingly accepts that responsibility. That is how he can both adapt himself to the inevitable and bring about meaningful change in his area of freedom.

I continued my letter to Marcia, this time in the spirit of both themes B (self-disclosure) and C 3 (reflection) of the master table:

Take a good look at yourself and the world in which you exist. Make the effort to perceive the crucial elements of your social being as projections of your own decisions. If you don't like the environment or the world in which you live, look at it as if it were your vomit. The world is your projection. It tells you what is inside. Only by distancing your insides from you, by reflecting on them rather than being them, can you achieve understanding of them and, with it, control over them.

For instance, the children fight, smoke marijuana, shoplift, and do poorly in school. Look at that as a reflection or result of the relation between you and Tim. Your children have "problems"; they manifest "symptoms." These are, for our philosophical purposes of self-disclosure, projections of the structure of your inwardness and therefore projections of your basic choices.

Let me put it otherwise. You cannot know what choices you are now making without the magnification and externalization rendered possible by the projection of your inward structure onto the screen that is your family life. This approach to self-disclosure can be painful. However, the pain is not a censor or a defense against the insight but by a direct experience of the freedom that you use in making the life-denying decision.

Go farther. Look at your marriage as a reflection of the person you have chosen yourself to be. More specifically, the details of your real life—details which trouble you—express your fundamental decisions about your relation to the world in general.

If you ask yourself four crucial questions about your objective life, you will have an outline of the basic decisions about who you are, what you expect, and what you deserve that you have incorporated into your self-definition. Let me be specific. Your sex-life, your marriage, your children, and your attitude about money are projections of your freely chosen self-definitions.

Let me concentrate on the last item. How do you feel about money? What is your financial situation and what are your financial problems? How do you feel about spending and earning money? Here you get a good clue of what your decisions have been regarding who you are and how you are to relate yourself to the society in which you live. It is now time to assume responsibility for these choices.

Anxiety

In two weeks I received this reply:

You were right. I thought about what you said in class and in your letter and I got very upset. I started to shake and felt my heart palpitate and my voice became tremulous. I did a lot of crying. I felt some relief. A lot of sobbing made me feel light and free.

Increase in the heartbeat, deepening of breathing, and a quavering voice are often responses to attack. Marcia's defenses are weakened. She is making a last-ditch fight for her very life. She is approaching the experience of the anxiety of her freedom. But she still fights the opening up of her own consciousness and with it the disclosure of her own freedom. However, the body's emerging reaction may indicate that she is losing the battle. Crying, which is often cathartic and relieving, means that Marcia has given up, has lost, has surrendered, has ceased struggling. She is in the process of relinquishing her old self-concept. That self-image has shown its bankruptcy. She is readying herself to receive the full disclosure of the power of her freedom. She is giving in to the recognition of her own freedom. That is why much of the tension is assuaged in weeping. The bodily anxiety (palpitations, hyperventilation, and quavering voice) is an earthquake in the person, where the subject, like Samson, tries desperately to hold up the collapsing building. The weeping is literally the melting of the world, the world becomes water.

Marcia continues:

You asked your questions: What has happened to your sex life, your marriage, your children, and your money since our first discussion? You asked me to rate myself on each item as, in my own eyes, improved, worsened, or unchanged. I am sorry to have to report that as my insight increased all four aspects of my life worsened.

We had a birthday party for our six-year-old girl. Tim and I had a big blow-up after the party. It spoiled everything for our daughter. Tim left and came home stone drunk. He was affectionate and wanted sex. I didn't. We had another noisy fight and again woke up the children. What am I to do?

Marcia

Marcia became transparent to herself by realizing that her sex life, her marriage, her children's behavior, and her management of money were compressed versions of her original decisions about the meaning of life and the nature of man; or, more specifically, her life reflects decisions about the meaning of *her* life and the nature of *her* self. Sex, marriage, children, and money were miniature replicas (projections) of Marcia herself. The fact that matters got worse and she got more upset are symptoms of *resistance against responsibility*.

The worsening of the key indices in her life could also be interpreted as the exacerbation of her general decision to say "no" to life; or, what is often the same, to say "yes" to herself by saying "no" to the representative of the other, or the objective pole in her life. In Marcia's case, the other was represented mostly by her family, and her saying "no" also included rejection of her parents. In any event, Marcia fought the surrender to the freedom that she is. She struggled bitterly against permitting herself the luxurious philosophic discovery that she is the creator of her world. That was the source of her upset.

What is in the way of Marcia's final insight that she is the god that creates her own fate? What is the insidious obstruction that prevents her access to the freedom that will change her life?

I wrote her back, and then discussed with the class, the following:

> *You are resisting the light of your own freedom. Your freedom scares you to death. You are holding on to the ignorance of your freedom. Let go. Have confidence that you can handle your own freedom. Your increased guilt, pain, and anger are resistances against responsibility. They are signs that you have not yet assumed responsibility for your being-in-the-world, for your bodily being or embodiment, or your empirical ego.*
>
> *You know what holds you back? What gives you grief? I think that you do not yet understand and believe that you choose your own values, that you choose your own self-definitions and your own world constitutions. You are still looking for clues from the world, from the expert. You want others to tell you who you are.*
>
> *Others may want to define you, but it is in the nature of things that they cannot. Once you recognize the reality of your own freedom for setting values and the fact that you need account only to yourself, a great weight will have been lifted. Your strained breathing will become deep and relaxed. And you are then ready to effect real changes in your life.*

Here, I was making use of such themes from the master table as C 7 (freedom), C 8 (life), C 9 (commitment), and C 14 (contradiction).

My letter to Marcia continued,

> *Don't react with guilt to what I say. Do not let me be simply another person who introduces external standards into your life. Previous standards have failed in that they have made you feel guilty. Do not look at existential philosophy as still another set of standards against which you can measure your performance.*
>
> *A philosophy of freedom removes all external standards. Whatever standards exist are those you yourself have chosen and those that follow from your philosophical essence (such as your freedom, your death, your field of consciousness, etc.). Philosophy is meant to set you free.*
>
> *For instance, are you really sure that your relationship with Tim is bad? That*

your children are growing up "deprived," "neurotic," and "unhealthy"? Are you positively convinced that your sex life is bad and your finances irresponsible? Is fighting good or bad? Is a noisy and emotional home worse than a subdued and quiet family?

You must first make decisions on each and every one of these values, on these definitions of the "proper" behavior of human beings. There are no expert and no absolute solutions. You can perceive your family situation in a new perspective if you experiment by redefining what you think is bad as being really good. You can make the deliberate effort to believe you have a good rather than a bad family. In this way you enhance your freedom by liberating yourself from external constraints.

One strength you will achieve by accepting rather than denying yourself is that you will translate your neurotic guilt into existential guilt. Neurotic guilt is the debilitating and desperate pain that you now feel. Existential guilt is the joyous liberation, the relaxed confidence which comes with the insight that your authentic freedom is the dawn of a new and a beautiful day.

BELLA

Here is a letter from Bella:

I seem not to be able to feel close to my stepdaughter, an intelligent, lovely looking girl, since she has been away at college. We have a cordial relationship via phone and letter but when she's around I seem to telegraph my distaste for her messy way of life and she seems to express contempt for me by her actions. We had what I considered a healthy relationship—I have had an assortment of stepmothers and a stepfather and I have tried to be a very good friend rather than a surrogate mother.

My stepdaughter has been a militant force in her university and recites the dogma. Once when I could bear it no longer I left the room. Another time when I felt she was interfering with the religious education of the younger children and also making health suggestions to them which I felt were unwise. I spoke sharply to her—something I'd never done before. She has written to her father that these and a few other incidents she has hoarded in 13 years bother her and she also would like to develop a closer relationship with me.

I hope that existential philosophy will help me to become more accepting of her life-style, her sexuality—both homo and hetero—without letting the younger siblings think this is the way to go.

My husband thinks I was wrong in leaving the room. He feels I showed a lack of concern for her values on my part—while I felt it to be just the opposite—I've been biting my tongue a lot over the years!

Sincerely,
Bella

Following is a brief existential diagnosis of Bella's problem, along with selected prescriptions. The diagnosis is based only on the sparse data her letter provides and was meant for illustrative class discussion.

At the risk of being accused of male chauvinism, I must nevertheless say that Bella's sentence "I hope that existential philosophy will help me to become more accepting of her life-style, her sexuality—both homo and hetero . . ." is a "typically" (and perhaps also beautifully) feminine response. It is accepting, accommodating, and yielding. *She* is going to change; not the world. She is going to make the adjustment, not the daughter or society with its new mores. She reacts; she does not act. Bella is not directive and self-affirming. She expects to accommodate herself to the decisions made by the external world.

In my earlier chapters on existential love and existential sex I tried to show that a woman need not lose her femininity by asserting herself. She can, for example, choose to affirm her individual integrity by being female. But in this particular situation, the inability for self-affirmation seems to be the source of the difficulty. Extrapolated, this attitude of accommodation and adjustment can eventually lead to taking drugs, such as tranquilizers, to adjust her body to an inauthentic environment.

Bella's attitude toward a solution is like fighting water and air pollution by breeding a new kind of human organism that can survive in poisonous filth rather than cleaning our rivers and the air above our cities. It is distressing to see people adjust to that which is universally accepted as evil and wrong rather than to stand up and fight for what they know as the truth.

Bella thinks that philosophy may help her to change color so she will better fit the house decor. She is like the lioness in the jungle who, having herself killed the prey, waits for the male to finish his meal— which may take hours—before she ventures to eat. Should she approach the lion prematurely, he will growl, and she will quickly have to submissively play dead and wait further. Existential philosophy has the opposite effect. It will encourage Bella to take responsibility for her passivity, and through that act become self-affirming.

If Bella, by her own lights, thinks she is right in her attitude about her daughter, she should act accordingly. And if she is wrong, she should change her actions. That is authenticity.

Self-Disclosure

Let us now explore her letter from the point of view of self-disclosure as a guide to meaning in life (theme B of the master table). Bella appears to be excessively dependent on the relation with her stepdaughter as the source of meaning in her life. Her compulsive need to have her stepdaughter like her is probably a clue to Bella's general being-in-the-world. Her great sensitivity to rejection is undoubtedly manifested in all her other relationships. But what she is really saying is "I am not liked because I do not like myself." Her self-concept says, "Others cannot like me because I am intrinsically unlikable."

This mode of her being-in-the-world involves inauthentic responses to themes C 4 (self-reliance), C 5 (individuality), C 6 (eternity), C 10 (love) and C 6a (reverence) of the master table. If Bella has constituted her world in an inauthentic way with respect to these five themes, then that inauthenticity will not manifest itself only in her relationship to her stepdaughter. In fact, that relationship is probably a confused image, as in a dream, of her relation to her husband, her mother and father, her children, and eventually to herself. The latter is, technically, the relation between her transcendental and empirical egos (theme A 2 of the master table). Her transcendental ego has rejected her empirical ego.

At a subsequent class demonstration, I guided Bella through the following fantasy to illustrate her self-rejection:

K: I want you to go through a guided daydream. Are you willing?

BELLA: Yes.

K: Close your eyes. You are in a deep forest on a path. No one else is near. You follow the path. You can see it wind ahead of you for a mile. Suddenly a speck of a figure approaches in the distance. You walk toward each other. The figure becomes a human being; then you notice it is a child. When you face each other on the path you recognize the child as you yourself when you were a child. You look at one another. Now say something to her!

Bella—eyes closed, leaning forward, tears dropping on her lap—finally speaks after a long pause:

BELLA: Move over, you bitch! (She sobs bitterly.)

K: The little girl, the little Bella, is now weeping . . . off the path. Now talk to her again.

BELLA: Come back!

K: She's still crying.

BELLA: Don't cry; it's all right.

K: She's still crying.

BELLA: I wipe off her tears.

K: She stopped crying, but she looks very unhappy; she is glum.

BELLA: You're OK, Bella.

K: She is still glum. Hug her!

BELLA: I'm hugging her.

K: Tighter.

BELLA: I'm holding her really tight.

K: Tell her, "I love you, Bella, little girl." Don't let go of her.

BELLA: I love you, I love you, I love you! (Breaks again into heavy sobs.)
K: Stay that way for as long as it feels right and good—hugging her, loving her, and weeping.

Bella has had the experience in which her transcendental ego (her pure, conscious, objectless inwardness) *accepts* her empirical ego (her personality structure), something she evidently had not done before. That is clear from the fantasy.

Let us now return to an examination of the problem with her stepdaughter. This analysis removes the locus of the problem from the stepdaughter, who is external (objective) to Bella's conscious center, to the inward freedom for world constitution of Bella herself. The problem is shifted from the empirical to the transcendental ego (master table theme A 2). Bella must find the way to personal self-disclosure. She must demand more of herself and less from her stepdaughter. I told her, referring to her stepdaughter, "Let her be. Fulfill yourself instead, in your own way, independently of her. Create a life for yourself and by yourself."

Unless a person can stand on his own two feet, that is, be fully and personally in charge of the meaning-finding function of his life, he is also not able to successfully relate to others. For Bella, as with all of us, good interpersonal relations begin with improved self-disclosing authenticity.

Self-Definition

One aspect of Bella's problem is her confused perception of it. Here again philosophy can help. Self-disclosure means clarity, lucidity, and transparency. Self-disclosure means honesty with oneself and directness with others. Such openness is usually respected, much to the surprise of timid souls. I told Bella, "Define yourself clearly to your stepdaughter. Let her know what you expect from her. You may first have to find out for yourself what her place really is in your life. You must make clear to her in what way you are an absolute limit to her." That communication is real and therefore is an expression of love in the sense of respect for and awareness of otherness. Such mutual reverential recognition carries with it a reciprocal guarantee.

I continued speaking with Bella, "Permit her to define herself to you. Let her know that (1) you respect her right to make her own choices, even in deep areas such as sex and religion and (2) you have different values and expect her to respect these as well." In other words, define yourselves to each other authentically: "You must have *mutual* respect for individuality and difference. You will then achieve what I called a transcendental love in the chapters on existential love. You will establish a transcendental connection in spite of the severe empirical or psychological differences between the two of you."

Bella must never endeavor to settle the issues separating her from her stepdaughter by argument; only by mutual respect—of which she can set the first example—can these contradicting values live together. They can agree that they have differences. To *have* differences is to be *antagonistic* on the empirical level, whereas to *understand* that they have differences is to be *unified* on the transcendental level. In this way anger becomes bearable and even acceptable; ordinarily most people get upset if others are angry. Let us examine the following exchange between Bella and her stepdaughter:

STEPDAUGHTER: I'm really mad at you.

BELLA: Why?

STEPDAUGHTER: I resent you, you meddle, you frustrate me. I admit I could learn to hate you!

BELLA: I am not angry with you. I want you to feel your anger and I want to share it with you.

STEPDAUGHTER: Don't try psychoanalyzing me.

BELLA: I'm not, I'm honest and sincere.

STEPDAUGHTER: Bullshit!

BELLA: I am not angry with you because I understand how you feel; in fact, I think you are right and I would feel the same in your shoes.

STEPDAUGHTER: I'm going to scream!

BELLA: Let's scream together. . . . Then tell me about your anger. What do you feel? What do you think? How angry are you? At whom?

Gradually Bella and her stepdaughter discuss the anger. They experience a transcendental love between them. They no longer relate on the level of their anger. It is important for every authentic individual to go through that experience, that is, the experience of looking at (reflecting on) anger rather than being the anger. This action is more effective if the anger that is thus distanced and reflected on is addressed by another to oneself. Bella clearly has acquired the strength of inwardness by the toleration of her stepdaughter's anger. To achieve an intimate connection while stepping back from an angry argument is the meaning of the epoche or of the transcendental reduction.

I made further specific suggestions to Bella: "Assume control over your world. Take charge of that which is yours—not of that which belongs to another." This means that Bella must set fair, rational, and realistic limits to her stepdaughter's operation in Bella's private zone, including the territory which is her home. The test of relevance is found in the word "enforceable." A limit is enforceable if it is within Bella's territory. If it is not enforceable, Bella is either transgressing her territory or she has lost control over her own life.

Next, Bella must make up her mind to enforce the limits she has set. That resolve must be categorical and consistent. If she can carry it out, she is indicating that she *means* these limits. And stated limits are real limits only if they are meant. To mean one's limits is not a function of will power but of knowledge, insight, truth, and honest conviction.

Finally, Bella must announce or promulgate her resolve. Often the manner of announcing carries in it, audible to those concerned, the degree to which the speaker means it. Husbands and wives and parents and children are tuned to that wave length and can pick up the seriousness of the intention.

Within these general guidelines Bella was able to begin reconstructing her life. The details of her solution are personal and do not concern us here. They are dependent on incidental details of her family life.

REMEMBER

1. Your world reflects the choices you have made.
2. The quality of your marriage, of your relation with your children, of your sex life, and of your financial affairs reflects *your* choices and *your* self-concept.
3. Anxiety is the experience of emerging freedom.
4. To be upset is often a sign of resisting responsibility.
5. A philosophy of freedom removes external standards of behavior and values.
6. What appears to be a bad marriage may in truth be a good marriage.
7. It is not necessary for a woman to be accommodating.
8. Learn to love the child in you. That child is your parent.
9. Anger between people is an empirical fact that can unite them transcendentally.

16
Existential Parenthood
Children Deserve to Be Happy

Let us move from an existential approach to marital problems to the more specific issue of raising children. There are a relatively few simple rules governing an existential approach to rearing children. These can be compressed into nine easily remembered principles, to be covered in three chapters.

1. Enjoy your children

The primary rule is to enjoy your children rather than to feel obligated to teach them. Love them, do not mold them. It is of course possible and often both necessary and desirable to transform family relationships from personal ones to professional ones. A mother may need to be a therapist to her children and a father may find it necessary to be their teacher. But in an authentic parent-child relationship, professional (one-way) rather than personal (two-way) relations are the exception rather than the rule. In a professional relationship the child is the object; in an encounter the child is the subject that is the other.

Existential theories of child-rearing follow from the field-of-consciousness theory of man. Child-rearing in accordance with the nature of consciousness is authentic because it is natural. Reach out to your children and treat them as subjects; do not raise them according to certain principles and laws, rules and theories, because if you do you are really treating them as objects and not as the subjects they truly are. Furthermore, rules can be violated and thus produce neurotic guilt. It is human to be inconsistent, and rules do not permit inconsistency. Also, our society encompasses conflicting rules, another situation that produces neurotic guilt. Love may be inconsistent, but it does follow the undulating natural motion of the field of consciousness; love is a river moving from one conscious center to another. If you enjoy your children—their companionship, their play, their needs, their love, their anger, their mimicking, and their straining efforts to grow up—then your being-in-the-world conforms to the intentional outward reaching movement of the field of consciousness.

Children of enjoying parents will reciprocate and enjoy their parents as well. If you naturally love your children, your being-in-the-world conforms to the intentional structure of meaning. You give meaning and reality to your children by loving them. You also express your essence as an encountering individual when you love rather than educate them: you meet each of them as a subjective consciousness, with the respect, awe, and dignity that is their due, rather than in a spirit of shaping them according to irrelevant, external, and preconceived material or behavioral standards. The openness that follows from love rather than rules produces the optimum environment for growth because it not only allows but also encourages heady self-expression and expansive self-transcendence. Openness is the experience of joy spread all around.

To love rather than rule presupposes in the parent a healthy reservoir of inner security and the resulting ability to let be. Love requires risk, courage, and peace of mind. Rules result from panic, anxiety, and the demand for excessive safety.

2. Teach authenticity to your child

There are two ways to teach authenticity to your child or children. The first is by example. If you are authentic, that is, if you incorporate in your life the elements of the master table, you will be assured of successful children because of your successful parenthood. Just as a tranquilizer does not cure a neurosis, so a rule or a technique does not cure inauthenticity. Authenticity is a matter of the rectitude of the heart and the probity of the center. Authentic children begin with an authentic inner self in the parent. This point cannot be overstressed.

Fortunately, authenticity makes being a parent, as it does everything else, rather easy. Being a good parent is a natural mode of being because authenticity is being natural. And "natural" means to exist in conformity with the essentials of the field-of-consciousness theory of man. You teach authenticity to your children by unfailingly showing them an authentic human being in operation. They will model themselves accordingly. Your children will respond to life's stresses as they have observed *you* manage these problems.

Through Existential Children's Stories

A second way of teaching authenticity to children is literally, didactically, academically. The growth-movement subculture is often and needlessly afraid of the intellectual, the conceptual, the "head trip." Children, like adults, can be taught and they can enjoy the process. The intellect is a gift that can help us to a better life. Let us not ignore or neglect it. Let us not show it any disrespect, as Luther did in his notorious indictment, "the whore reason." He also wrote, "Reason is the greatest enemy that faith has: it never comes to the aid of spiritual things" (*Table Talk*, 1569). The intellect, with its ability to create abstract concepts, can give both parents and children a direct and economical, that is, time-saving and mnemonic, image of the authentic individual. Feelings and experiences can be forgotten. An abstract concept, easy to record and recall, can help us recapture the experience and its meaning.

How can we teach the existential principles of authenticity didactically and conceptually to little children? Let us look at an example.

Dr. Seuss' book for children, *Horton Hears a Who,* is an excellent illustration of the didactic, child-oriented approach to themes C 6 (eternity), C 6a (reverence), C 9 (commitment) and C 9a (Reality) in particular.

The Whos are invisibly small peoplelike creatures who are threatened with destruction by the animals in the jungle, who do not believe in their existence. Horton, the huge elephant, is determined to save the Whos because all individuals are valuable even though they may be insignificantly small. The Whos can be saved only if they make themselves heard, that is, if they reach the other (C 9, commitment and C 9a, Reality). They must convince the animals of the forest that they in fact do exist. In order to be heard, to announce that they exist, and to be in touch with what is real, all the Whos scream and holler in unison, but the huge and threatening jungle animals cannot hear them. Finally, the littlest Who, hardly visible even in the world of Whos, saves the day because in adding his voice to all those already shouting he breaks the catastrophic barrier of silence between the Whos and the animals. In this way, the littlest of the little Whos resolves the tension, overcomes the danger, and saves the lives of all. The smallest succeeds in reaching others, in creating communication, in making everyone heard, and in touching what is real.

This approach is one way to demonstrate to a child the truth of the fact that above all *each individual consciousness is extraordinarily important.* In the story the salvation of mankind was brought about by what on the surface appeared to be the most insignificant individual of all. Even that individual is an infinite consciousness.

With some imagination it is possible to engender a plethora of existentially didactic children's stories. Following are a few suggestions on
how a parent or teacher might proceed, using children's stories as a
vehicle, in teaching to a child the essentials of a field-of-consciousness
theory of man.

Story Writing

The symbols of the story should be objects with which the child easily
identifies. Each child is different. One child loves pumpkins, so his
parents can make up a story in which the individuals are pumpkins.
Another likes baseball. For him, a story can be constructed whose hero is
either the equipment—such as the baseball bat which every player rejected until its true worth was "discovered"—or a player with a similar
fate. However, it is my belief that symbols which are somewhat distant
from the obvious target of identification, the child—baseball *bats* rather
than *people*—go more readily past the defenses of the child's ego to
touch directly his deeper nature as a field of consciousness.

Another point to keep in mind is the necessity to ascertain the
existential theme for which the child is ready or for which he has the
greatest need. One child may have very low self-regard, and a story about
the indestructible right to exist—such as *Horton*—may be to the point
for him. Details aside, the story is derived from theme C 6 (eternity) of
the master table. Another may feel isolated, and a story underscoring
the naturalness—the inevitability, the beauty and the ease—of connectedness among people and even among all living things may be helpful. Such
a story would be derived from themes A 1 (field theory) and C 9 (commitment) of the master table. To a child needing confidence in self-
expression, a story that illustrates theme B (self-disclosure) may be meaningful. As a matter of fact, ministers, priests, and rabbis can get ideas
from these generating principles for parables having a moral, to insert
in their sermons.

The connectedness theme might be illustrated through a tree that is
lonely, first, because it is rooted and thus stationary and, secondly, because it is separated, disconnected, and alienated from the trees around
it. One day, a rabbit, in digging a hole, helps the estranged tree to make
the philosophic discovery that the trees around it are in truth part of
himself in that they are but shoots from one common parent root. All
trees are brothers; they embrace each other and are joined in their subterranean reality. The rabbit, so thoroughly foreign and untreelike, was
the messenger of the gods, bearing the truth of the unity of all trees as
a by-product of its independent activity.

For children the philosophical theme of self-expression (theme C 13—
growth) can be illustrated by a sun afraid to shine—which in its shyness

blackens and freezes the solar system, previously vibrant with life—or by a river too shy to flow or afraid of losing its water by flowing, which thereby dries the reservoirs and fields and kills the vegetation. Self-expression is the nature of the sun and the essence of the river. Without its luminosity the sun does not exist, and without the flow the riverbed is dry. Furthermore, with the new light joy returns to the planet and life returns to the vegetation upon the renewed flow of the river.

Growth, time, self-transcendence, and, in general, the field-of-consciousness theory of man, can be translated into children's stories. If the theory is correct, such translation is likely to touch a responsive unconscious string and make it vibrate to the harmony of existence.

3. Have space and time for love

A third prescription for authentic parenthood is to have space and time for love. To be human is to be "in time," or simply to be "time" or "temporal." But it is also to be "space" and have territory. I am my lived time as well as my lived space. Raising children is not a chore, task, or duty. It is living. And living means to allow the sense of one's time to be felt and one's space to become real and conscious. Time *means* room, territory, space, relaxation, and unhurriedness. It means time to be, time to let be, and time to be with. Modern life has deadlines and efficiency experts, schedules, and time-budgeting. Today time is perceived as a thing, to be cut up and organized, apportioned and proportioned, divided, multiplied, and added up. These are operations performed on objects, not on human subjectivities. Time, like consciousness itself, is a continuous and peaceful field. Objectifying it does violence to it.

The same considerations apply to space. Space is continuous and unitary. It cannot be cut up. Only objects can be cut and their parts separated. Walls and partitions do not cut up space. They exist in space, a space that remains continuous and unitary. Your children are part of your space and time. They are the movement of you and the extension of you in the sense in which space and time make your movement possible and comprehensible. Your children are your space and your time; they are the outward pointing and outward reaching, the self-transcendence, of you. They are your arms reaching further into the distance of your own space, and they are your feet carrying your whole body to new spaces that are your spaces. Your children are your doors and windows to the world.

The message to the authentic parent is, "Let your child be, let yourself be, and love one another. Move in the direction of your child; move with your child. Loving children is natural." Translated into the terminology of philosophy, that statement becomes, "Permit the time that you are to unfold itself naturally, and move into the space that you are, naturally." Your children temporalize and spatialize you. They are now your arms and legs. If you love them, you are your space-time. If you are alienated from them, you have isolated yourself from your own space-time. In a word, love blooms in the internal peace bereft of external deadlines and borders.

Time for love means also space for love. Overpopulated living conditions do not provide the leisurely space within which love of your children is given an opportunity to grow. Our society has become well aware of this fact, and he who escapes from the inner city to the wilderness commune demonstrates enviable wisdom. If people live like bees, busy and congested, they cannot move toward one another. The authentic parent must create space and time in his life for his children—vacations, evenings, weekends. He must make himself available and he must *want* to be available. However, availability does not come from time-budgeting. It comes from psychological focus, from a relaxed existence, and from commitment to children.

To the authentic parent, his children are more important than his job or his hobby, more important than his pleasure and his ambition. He therefore creates in his own life a large psychological space and a vast amount of psychological time—both at home and on the job. That psychological space-time is then filled by his children. The authentic parent does not come home exhausted, nor does he spend his weekends in collapse because he overextended himself during the week. The authentic parent looks forward to time spent with his children because that is the space and time that he in truth and in reality actually is. When with his children he is but being himself.

But the child also has his own space, independent of the spaces of his parents and siblings. And that unique space gives the child dignity.

4. Recognize the dignity of the child

The next existential rule for authenticity in child-rearing is to recognize the dignity of the child. The authentic parent accepts the uniqueness and the dignity of each child. He respects his individual differences and idiosyncrasies. The authentic parent realizes that themes C 5 (individuality) and C 6a (reverence) apply to his child from earliest infancy on. An authentic parent perceives the constitutional guarantees with which his child is born. He respects the child's "unalienable rights" even in the crib.

What practical arrangements follow if parents recognize the dignity of their child? For one thing, a child is given privacy. He has his own bed and his own room, if at all possible. No one, child or adult, enters his room without first knocking and receiving permission. Nothing is rearranged and no drawers opened without his permission. It is clearly established early in the child's life that there is a space which is his exclusively, which he can arrange as an inviolate extension of his personality. There is also a time that is his, that represents him, and that no one preempts. He has chores and assignments, but there is a time that he can count on having and that he knows no one will violate. Time and space can be combined in a reasonable allowance which is his to spend or to save as he wishes. There can be no qualifications to his use of the sphere of being that is his alone (except the rules of law, safety, and health).

Furthermore, to recognize the dignity of the child means that his opinions are respected and his needs are heard. A child is never ridiculed. If a baby wants to suck his thumb, that is recognized as a legitimate need, and it is respected. If he has a bottle or a blanket beyond the age at which his parents are comfortable with it, he has a right to have that need recognized. His feelings are consulted and his opinions sought in family decisions. He is given freedom with the clothes he wears, the manner in which he styles his hair, etc.

The authentic parent does not project any of his own expectations onto the individuality of his child. The parent knows the child needs opportunities, but he cannot push him in the direction of sports or music, dancing or mathematics, just because in the opinion of the parent that is where life's meaning is to be found. To raise a child authentically is to "educate" him (to allow him to "lead himself out"). A parent must provide plenty of opportunities, space for movement, but no coerced directions. That is why an authentic parent is an authentic individual first. The freedom he engenders in the child is threatening to the inauthentic parent. Only the authentic parent has overcome the anxiety of confronting the freedom of man, with its plethora of possibilities.

The only legitimate expectation that the authentic parent has of his child is that the child himself be authentic. He wants his child to grow up fulfilled and happy, free and rich in potential. The authentic parent extends the recognition to his child that is the rightful due of any human subjectivity. He loves his child with proper regard for the inviolable otherness of a separate individual. The authentic parent loves his child in accordance with theme C 10 of the master table (love, encounter).

The desiderata for love described in the chapters on love apply not only to lovers but to all loving human relationships. Preeminent among these are parent-child relationships. I believe that the parent-child connection is far deeper and longer lasting than any relationship between adults, such as that between man and wife. As an exercise, you should go back to chapters 2, 3, 4, and 5 and ask yourself, in connection with every one of the nine themes, "Am I expressing that in my relation with my child?" And if the answer should be "no," then ask yourself,

"How can I translate that particular requirement of authentic love into the relationship I have with my child?"

5. Give authentic love

Mirroring, for example, can be achieved by honest conversations on a level the child can understand. A parent should share with his child all aspects of his life about which the child asks. No questions need be avoided.

The conquest-surrender element of authentic love can be expressed in the parent-child relationship in a variety of ways. It can be manifested in simple activities, such as games and sports, which involve both conquest and surrender (winning and losing). It can also be shown in the unqualified commitment, the decision to care, which a parent can demonstrate to his child.

Adulthood and resistance can be integrated into the parent-child relationship in terms of demands and expectations for mature behavior and responsible attitudes made by the parent. The parent's message to his child in connection with this theme of existential love is "Be independent," "Do it on your own," "Don't ask me," "Don't depend on me," and "I don't care how you do it."

Finally, the element of worship (see chapter 2) is represented by the total lack of resentment that the authentic parent feels toward his child. Worship is the open joy at having children, regardless of the pains that accompany this process. The meaning of worship in existential child-rearing requires further analysis, which however cannot be carried out here.

The fact that the parent's love of his child shares the characteristics of all love is not to say that the authentic parent perceives his child as merely another adult. Not at all. First of all, a child is *not* an adult but a child, and, second, relations with children cannot be dropped like adult relationships. The specific difference that characterizes the parent's love for his child is that it is an *absolutely irrevocable commitment*. All other human commitments are relative, conditional, qualified, and reversible. The commitment the authentic parent makes to his child, however, is a unique kind of love: It is an unqualified, categorical, absolute, and unconditional commitment—one that cannot be broken.

Such total security is the soil on which the child grows. Unconditional parental commitment is the world that the parent creates for the child as he creates the child. The authentic parent makes an absolute commitment not because it is good for the psychological development of the child, but because through this act he defines himself as a parent. Without that act he is not a parent. In short, the absolutely irrevocable nature of being a parent is the one ingredient in parental love that is not found in other types of love.

The following item from a newspaper illustrates an absence of the commitment that defines a person as a parent:

CAN YOU PROVIDE A HOME FOR
THESE TWO MOTHERLESS CHILDREN?

Can you take into your home two motherless Jewish children who need love, care, and Jewish education?

The _____ County Department of Social Services describes the children as an attractive, cooperative, 10-year-old girl who is an honor roll student, and an outgoing, exuberant, 11-year-old boy with strong leadership qualities.

After their mother died two years ago, the children's father placed them in a foster home because his work requires him to travel a great deal. Now he wants to move them to another home because the present foster parents cannot accept his desire to have the children receive a Jewish education.

The Department is looking for foster parents who can keep this boy and girl for three years, until the father is able to retire from his job. Anyone who can provide a home for these or other children should call _____.

Not much comment is needed on this story. Nevertheless, there is little evidence of commitment on the part of the father, and this at a time—the death of the children's mother—when his commitment should be increased. It appears that these children will find it difficult to know the meaning of a home, even to the extent of knowing what it means to be homeless. These two children may never understand the homelessness of man, because the philosophical idea of a home—although never fulfilled totally for anyone—was never really clarified for them in childhood by an absolute commitment from their surviving parent.

6. Accept your dignity as a parent

There is another, altogether different side to the matter of accepting the dignity of your child—accepting your own dignity as a parent as well. You as a parent have needs exactly comparable to those of your child. You also need privacy, need to have your dignity respected, and must have the opportunity to express the integrity of your values. For your sake and for the sake of your child, you must insist that your legitimate and rational needs become the limits to your child. As a parent you must have the space-time that is yours exclusively, as is also true of your child or children. By respecting your own private and personal needs, you likewise teach your child to respect his.

Do not *use* your child—for your happiness, satisfaction, or any other needs (the extreme manifestation of this would be incest)—but *meet him.* Recognize in him an authentic otherness. But do the same for yourself. Do not use yourself in the sense of sacrificing yourself needlessly for your child. Meet *yourself* in the same reverential and respectful transcendental manner in which you are expected to meet your child. Do not permit your child to use you.

Let me now turn briefly to a corollary point in this exposition of an authentic parent-child relationship. If the relationship has been authentic, then the child's move away from home is easy. In an authentic parent-child relationship, the teens present no unusual problem. As an example, let me take what to some may appear to be an extreme. Parent and child are extremely angry at each other and have the following succinct interchange.

TEENAGER: "I hate you so much that I could kill you!"

PARENT: "So could I."

If we assume an authentic and not a pathological or inauthentic parent-child relationship, we can translate the above capsule transaction into the following:

TEENAGER: "I am more myself, more independent, more self-reliant than you seem to realize. Here—feel my otherness, my individuality, my independence!"

PARENT: "I really hear you! I truly sense in you a full-fledged, independent individual. I like, respect and admire what I see! You have freed me as well. I can and want no longer to be dependent on you. My meanings have to be found in me and not in you!"

The breaking off between parent and child in the teens is no problem if the authenticity of the family was assured during the formative years. If a problem does exist, it is a symptom of the fact that the guidelines were not followed. A generalized prescription is to make an effort to accelerate the shift of freedom from parent to child, to hurry the process of growth toward authenticity. That can be accomplished didactically, that is, academically and intellectually, as well as psychotherapeutically (through emotional self-disclosure and experiential transparency). Psychotherapy must be viewed as an important adjunct to philosophic self-disclosure and growth.

REMEMBER

1. The authentic parent enjoys his children.
2. It is more important to love your children than it is to educate them.

3. Children are taught authenticity through the example of the parent's authenticity.

4. Children can be taught authenticity through imaginative stories based on the themes of the master table.

5. Make up existential parables and tell them to your child.

6. The authentic parent organizes his life to create ample space and time for love.

7. Your children are your arms and your legs. They reach out for you into the world.

8. The authentic parent respects the dignity of his child. He recognizes the child's need for privacy and he listens to the child's opinions.

9. The authentic parent expresses the characteristics of existential love (such as mirroring, conquest-surrender, adulthood, resistance, and worship) in his relation to his child.

10. Each parent must respect his own dignity equally as much as that of his child.

17
Existential Parenthood
Your Limits Are Real

The existential personality theory is not only a philosophy of the freedom of consciousness, it is also a philosophy about the severe and implacable limits imposed upon consciousness. The authentic parent possesses an accurate philosophic understanding of the meaning of limits.

7. Be clear about the meaning of limits

The seventh rule for authentic parenthood is be clear about absolute limits. The authentic individual does not—in his everyday affairs such as matters of family life—assume personal responsibility, blame, or guilt for the boundaries that surround life. But he does assume responsibility for dealing with those boundaries realistically. As an authentic parent you must, therefore, distinguish between those limits which *you* have set and for which you consequently hold yourself accountable and those limits set by *nature* for which you have chosen *not* to assume responsibility, because you *are not* responsible.

Your first task is to recognize real or natural limits. Articulate them; announce them; discuss them; state them; admit them; accept them. Second, proclaim loud and clear to the world—loud enough so that you can hear yourself—that you are not responsible (not to blame) for the nature of things. You are not God; you have not created the world; and you refuse and reject having others define you into a position of responsibility for situations not of your making and not within your territory of control. You reject all responsibility for setting these limits. You reject responsibility in your own mind, and you inform others that you will rebel against their possible implications of responsibility.

A parent who sets limits for his child or the partner of a marriage who limits either himself or his spouse need not feel that in truth *he* or *she* is personally creating those limits. The parent or partner "sets" limits only in the sense that he *reports* the limits that he knows already exist, independently of choice, with no responsibility on his part.

Financial structures are a good example. In families where the demand for money is greater than the supply *and* where husband and wife are reasonably responsible regarding earnings and expenditures, bitter quarrels nevertheless often develop about financial matters. The economy and the limitations of job and profession are boundaries that cannot be readily transcended. And it is indeed the height of inauthenticity to blame the wife or the husband or the children for these frustrating limits. The family should speak, in effect, with one voice, these words: "Our needs are facts and our economic situation is a fact. We can all love one another, understand one another, and support one another, accosted as we are by a common enemy." If they cannot utter these words, then it is ignorance of limits, not ill will, that obstructs them. A person who assumes responsibility for that which is not his is like a straw that moves with the wind—he is the slave of every man, he has no center, and lacks any sense of solidity.

Let me be specific. Each authentic individual, and in particular each authentic parent, must say to himself, "I am not responsible for the nature of the world. If the weather is bad, I am not at fault. I am not responsible for history, for geography, or for economics. I am not responsible for what my ancestors did or did not do. I am not responsible for society. I do not take either the blame or the credit for the actions or inactions of people who look like me, talk like me, are related to me, live near me, work or go to school with me, etc. I did not create the social problems with which we live today, although I hold myself responsible for doing my share to ameliorate them.

"Neither am I responsible for my body. I will not tolerate ridicule nor will I feel ashamed of that which results from genetic programming and is forever beyond the reach of my free will. That includes color, size, proportions, attractiveness, unattractiveness, deformities, etc. I will not accept competition on this level, except as necessary functionally.

"I must of course remember that to reject responsibility for undesirable limits implies an equal rejection for what we might call desirable limits. I cannot accept praise for beauty or intelligence nor for strength and talent, because these qualities are beyond the region of my free will. I am to be blamed or praised, however, for what I do or do not do with these limits. I cannot be blamed for a talent that I do not possess, but I am responsible for a talent which I do not develop."

It is as inauthentic for a person with a crippled body to feel guilty, inadequate, or self-conscious over that fact as it is for a person with a harmonious and athletic body to feel self-confident, superior, and arrogant because of these genetic accidents.

The absolute character of these limits and the total lack of personal responsibility for them is an incontrovertible fact and a freeing fact. But this important fact of life is not known inherently. A two-fold decision to know it and to act on that knowledge is required. It is the responsibility of parent and teacher to inform children not only of facts about obsidian rocks and mollusks, but also of the unalterable limits that existence imposes on man. And the child must learn, "You are not responsible for these limits. Face them, yes; but do not say you created them and that therefore you are a lesser person because of these limits."

Praise, like blame, must always be directed at the zone of freedom. When you praise a girl for being pretty or a boy for being tall you are really sending out to him the following insidiously inauthentic message: "You are to be praised for that over which you have no control—your physical beauty or your physical size. You are in luck at the moment, but beware of tomorrow, since you are in constant danger that some other factors external to your free will may be discovered, and those will then imprison you because they are limits." The price we pay to be free of undeserved guilt is that we abandon also undeserved praise.

Because understanding limits is central to existential parenthood, it is necessary to explore specific limits in some detail.

PARENTS ARE LIMITS

A most important limit for the child is the set of parents he is born with. Each set of parents represents a unique set of limits. A child must be informed appropriately of that unalterable fact.

Take Janet, for example. Today, she is in her early twenties, unhappily married, childless (her twenty-four-year-old husband had a vasectomy), and feels lost in a sea of meaninglessness. She feels unworthy and incomplete. Her father abandoned her mother and her when Janet was less than a year old. Further, he left the country to avoid alimony. For all practical purposes, Janet does not have a real father. Her mother remarried when Janet was four. Soon she had a half-brother, who was preferred ("naturally," as Janet innocently and ignorantly put it to me) by her stepfather. Her stepfather was cruel, distant, and unfair like the stepmother in *Cinderella*. Her parents fought over her, since her mother often stood up for Janet's rights. When Janet was nine and her half-brother five, her stepfather asked her to take the little boy for a walk. He was hit by a passing car and died a few hours later in the hospital.

Janet never got over this trauma. For the rest of his life, the stepfather blamed her for the death of his son. On his deathbed his last words were the same old refrain: "You killed my only son. I hate you for it. You are polluted and you will never be forgiven. You will be punished in hell."

Let us now articulate Janet's existential limits as far as these relate to her parents.

Janet's limits, as a young child, fall into five categories: (1) a father who abandoned her; (2) a stepfather who rejected her; (3) a half-brother who died; (4) guilt piling on from all directions; and (5) a weak but accepting mother. Early in life Janet accepted personal responsibility and blame for her parents' behavior. Not only did her childhood problems truncate her development (which is a separate issue), they also convinced her she was less of a person because of the kind of family situation in which she lived. For instance, she accepted sole responsibility for the accidental death of her brother. Also, she accepted responsibility for her father's abandonment: She convinced herself that she deserved to be abandoned, like a rotten piece of fruit.

At twenty-two, very little can be done to change the formative years. However, even ten or fifteen years earlier, the message could have been given by a teacher, a relative, or even one of the parents. And the message should have been "Your parents are your limits. You have no responsibility for the existence of these limits. You have lousy parents. That is bad enough. But that's the way they are; it's not your fault; their inadequacy is not a punishment for you. You deserve better because you are human and all humans deserve better. Don't blame yourself for your parents. Neither should you hide what they are doing to you from your friends. Share your sorrow with them. Bad parents are not an embarrassment to you—unless you hold yourself responsible for them. Bad parents are an embarrassment only to themselves."

Janet's case is of course extreme. In less severe situations, the insight conveyed to a child that his parents are limited and that therefore he is not responsible for their defects is a soothing, simplifying, and strength-giving truth to him. Seeing his life in this new light, the child can adjust to the inauthenticity of his parents as he can to bad weather or any other disappointment.

THE PHYSICAL WORLD IMPOSES LIMITS

The limits of the physical world, of so-called nature, are illustrated by mountain or rock climbing. An educated authentic person does not assume responsibility for the existence of gravity and for the resistance the mountain or cliff presents to his progress. A good climber has integrated into his being a healthy respect for the unavoidability of the limits imposed on him by the external reality to which he relates. In fact, we can *define* a professional climber as one whose behavior derives from respect for gravity. Rock climbing is an excellent lesson in philosophy. It teaches the reality of the other, the absoluteness of limits that bind and border human existence. And it shows that there is health and joy in meeting a challenge.

The seasoned rock climber does not question the authority of his limits. He is not bothered by them; he is not upset by them. He does not assume personal responsibility for their existence. He does not blame himself for the difficulty of the task. But rock climbing is also pleasurable and inspiring. It teaches that man is fulfilled, that he finds his meaning, through the other. The statement "I climb the peak because it is there" means "I love otherness because conquering *it* makes *me* feel the muscles of my existence. In conquering the mountain I do not overcome it or surpass its resistance. On the contrary, I embrace the mountain. We are one."

SOCIETY IS A LIMIT

Society is another factor in life which imposes limits. These occur mostly in the form of injustice. The authentic parent recognizes the existence of these limits; he shares these facts with his children; he transmits that knowledge to them. *The authentic parent does not assume personal responsibility for the existence of these limits,* and he acts accordingly. Injustice, inequality, and unfairness are realities in all societies, worse in some than in others. Of course, you must teach your child to fight injustice, to stand up for his rights; but along with this, you must clarify the *price* or *danger* of his affirming justice: He will probably lose his fight. But, as a result of the child's understanding these facts about social reality, realistically, his determination to struggle must be increased through hope for success and not diminished through fatalism about failure.

In all social classes children encounter physical dangers from bullies, hoodlums, and irresponsible drivers. Little children playing in the street, riding tricycles, bigger ones on bicycles, and even larger ones in cars are all vulnerable to the threat of irresponsible, stupid, sadistic, drugged, or psychopathic drivers. That threat is a limiting social fact to the parents and to the children. It is, in the inner city, but also in suburbia, a threat of often dire proportions. The fact that a child has a *right* to use the streets, the *right* to safety, does not mean that he can push back society's limits to make legitimate room for himself and survive at the same time.

THE FAMILY IS A LIMIT

We must add to this set of social limits another one. The child's playmates may have parents who refuse—out of their irresponsible torpor—

to recognize these limits. The child's peers thus exert pressure to ignore limits, which is then but another limit in turn. Let us witness a typical parent-child discussion (rewritten for philosophic purposes) which illustrates several of the points regarding limits made up to now. Bob is a twelve-year-old boy.

BOB: Mother, I'm biking over to the Speedy for a Slurpee.

MOTHER: You know, Bob, that you are not permitted to cross the avenue on your bike.

BOB: Stop treating me like a baby, Mother!

MOTHER: We have an absolute rule in this house about biking across the avenue.

BOB: Just because your parents were overprotective you don't have to take it out on your own children! What's more, I'm going with Lou.

MOTHER: What about Mrs. L, Lou's mother? Lou *is* your age, you know.

BOB: They treat him like a grown-up. He doesn't have to ask. He's not stifled.

MOTHER: I'm sorry, Bob. Listen closely to me, since I'm not repeating myself. Here are my final words: (1) You and I are both stuck with the dangers of the avenue. I can't change that problem and don't you ask me to, either. You might as well ask me to change the laws of physics.

(2) Maybe I'm overprotective; I don't know what that means. Unfortunately, you've got only one mother and I'm the one. I've got my limitations, and it's about time you realized and accepted them. I'm trying to accept yours.

(3) Each family has different standards and a different definition of responsibility. The conflicting values between ours and Lou's family are rough limitations on you, Bob. Lou's family—by their very existence—puts pressure on you, Bob. That's a fact. Lou's your friend and I assume no responsibility for that. His friendship is a limit to you.

I know, Bob; these are facts that limit me too. I won't argue, because you don't argue with facts.

(4) I am deeply sympathetic with the pain and frustration that these worldly limits cause you. I'll weep and complain and scream *with* you, Bob, never *at* you! I, like you, suffer from the same limiting facts. I love you."

Bob's mother is alluding to three limits: physical danger, parental limitations, and social pressures. As I mentioned earlier, one of the most severe limitations facing a child are his parents. But the parent need not assume responsibility for being a limit to his child. For instance, a parent need not feel that he must be perfect. The authentic parent accepts his limitations, and if that act is sincere, it will transfer with ease to the child. It is healthy for the parent to accept his limitations just as it is necessary for his child to accept that finitude. Each parent has certain neuroses. He must not feel guilty because of them, nor must he feel necessarily inadequate as a parent because, like most people, he displays a number of neurotic behavior patterns. The imperfect parent can be direct with his child: "That is how I am. I don't like it. It makes *both* our lives difficult. But it is no tragedy. We can both accept it. We are all a little crippled; let us be understanding and accepting, not bitter and vindictive."

Children are never too young to learn about limits. Of course, I mean realistic limits, not cruel and unreasonable ones. The precise definition of *reasonable* in this context is difficult to state. I do not want to justify mean, vicious, and irresponsible behavior by parents, nor do I condone the neurotic or sadistic use of children. I am discussing here reasonable parents who feel guilty because of their "normal" human inadequacies. It is their responsibility not to use their own limits to truncate the joy they can have in their children. A responsible parent will never say, "My human limits give me an excuse to fail." He will not say either, "I must overcome my limits," because that is simply to repeat, "My human limits give me an excuse to fail!" The authentic parent says, "I accept my limits; I love myself in spite of or because of them."

Another common parental limitation worth repeating here is the economic strictures on the family. Some families have more money than others. A child is severely limited by the lack of opportunity that a low economic status implies. That is a fact that must be clearly brought before the child (as well as the parent). A realistic appraisal of the family's economic situation is a basic health rule. As the parent learns to cope with his financial strictures—either by responsibly adjusting his life-style to his economic possibilities or by working hard to increase the family income—so will his child. Any limit recognized as such can be an authentic source of character and strength and need not be an excuse for human failure and personal inauthenticity.

Families can also fail dismally through external or internal causes such as death, disability, nervous breakdowns. Emergency preparations are needed—a readiness to face the limiting factor that is *fate,* the unexpected, the calamitous. The authentic parent copes with the limits of fate by sharing with his child the following insights: "I do *not* assume responsibility for the existence of this disaster (fire, flood, death, economic recession, illness, etc.). I *do* assume responsibility for coping with it successfully. Coping is something we do together—it is a *with* activity, not one against each other. The disaster unites us; it does not pit us against each other."

Another significant limit which children confront is the value-system of their parents. A parent need not change his values, but he must share with his child the fact that his idiosyncratic values are indeed a limit on the child. Although the parent realizes this, he will stick to his values. The child can adjust to that truth. He learns from it that he also has the right to his own value-system. Some parents are ultraliberal; others, ultraconservative. Some are religious; others, atheistic. Some are warm and permissive; others, coldly rational and authoritarian. Some set education as the highest goal; others, sport. Some stress morality; others, success. It is understandable and right that parents wish to transfer their values to their children. However, problems result; a good illustration of one is Richard's religious conflicts.

Richard

Richard is thirty-five, married, with three children. He is a college graduate and works in elementary education. The overall impression he made on me at our first meeting was that of a person who has "guilt" written all over him. He perceives himself as totally inadequate. This, of course, is not to say he *is* inadequate.

Richard's inauthenticity appears to result from religious conflicts based in childhood. He told me he was brought up in a strict Catholic environment and that he had recently shed his religious commitments. He no longer goes to church or to confession, and as a result, he feels he is a poor father and husband, etc. In short, Richard is unable to cope with the value-system of his parents. His education and his reason prompted him to reject his parents' religious training and its rules. But his body and nervous system still resonate to the harmonies of the absolute values of his childhood and to the inflexible dogmas of his childhood home.

I felt Richard could be helped by recognizing that indeed he had a religious and a philosophical—that is, a theological—problem. And that this problem had to be resolved in theological and not psychiatric terms.

For Richard, talk of God and consciousness is more relevant to his authentic life processes than talk of sex, Oedipus, parents, and toilet training. Thus, if there is an anodyne to Richard's pain, it can probably be found in the message of existential theology. If Richard becomes a philosopher, if he understands the connection between God and consciousness, then he may achieve reconciliation and be both a religious Catholic and a modern man at the same time. The dogmas and rules of his early home may now be perceived by him as the only possible and acceptable *symbols* for expressing life's most profound philosophical realities. Religious truths are only symbolic, but for Richard they are the only way to deal with his ultimate philosophic concerns.

How to Choose Values for Your Children

I use the case of Richard to show parents how to avoid such perhaps incurable problems regarding values and religious commitments in the future adulthood of their children. There are two basic considerations to keep in mind.

First, children need guidance in the selection of values. It is the responsibility of parents to make value-choices for their children. It is the function of the parent to establish in his own life and then in that of his children the values and goals that will give direction to the life of the family. In adopting a firm posture with respect to values, a parent sends a triple message to his children:

1. An authentic person makes decisions. The child learns the meaning of being a subjectivity. An authentic subjective and free inwardness, that is, a bona fide person, *can* and *does* choose values. In witnessing an unequivocal religious commitment, the child meets an authentic decision-maker and value-chooser in the person that is his parent. The example is his teacher. "If Mom and Dad can use their freedom to make commitments, so can I." That is what the child has learned. One child learns that when you face a conflict you get drunk. Another child learns that when in conflict you make a decision. We learn how to make a commitment only by observing our model make a commitment. And what we observe above all is the fact that a commitment is a human *possibility* and not that commitment must be made to one or another specific religious persuasion. These are the basic teachings of life that children can really learn only from their parents.

2. A second lesson taught the child through the parent's clear commitment to a specific value-system is that the freedom of another person is everyone's irrevocable limit. The child learns the meaning of the object or of the objective pole of the intentional field that is the stream of human consciousness. He discovers that the hardest substance in this world is not a diamond but the freedom of another consciousness. That discovery is the basis of the democratic way of life and government. The child respects the rights of others, and with that respect comes an equal reverence for his own freedom. In an authentic family, the child discovers the adamantine hardness of his parent's value-system and thereby experiences the power of another freedom. The freedom of the parent is the impenetrable other in his experience. However, in the same authentic family, the child learns that he also possesses the power of his free choice of values. His choices as the years mature him can be as adamantine as those of his parents.

3. Finally, the child, through direct experience, learns of a second limit: the existence of values. The first limit was the existence of freedom in the

subjectivity of his parents. Values are life-styles, ideals, goals, and roles. If Whitehead was right when he wrote that all of Western philosophy is a footnote to Plato, then Plato's insight is the key to Western culture. And what was Plato's intuition? It was the fact that values exist objectively. Ideals, including values, exist independently of human perception. The existing ideals are thus a nonnatural (that is, a nonphysical) limit to man. We may reject these ideals, we may ignore them, we may protest that they are unattainable, but they remain to haunt us. It is both unrealistic and impractical to close our eyes to the reality of ideals. That is the second philosophical limit to human existence taught experientially to the child when he perceives his parent's values as limits to his life.

All these factors were present in distorted fashion in Richard's childhood. His parents, as do many or most, committed a grievous error: They confused free choice with absolute truth. Instead of sending to Richard the *inauthentic* message: "The Church is the absolute and final truth"—which permanently damaged his personality—they should have sent him the *authentic* message: "I (or we) freely choose the Church to be the absolute and final truth." The former is a vise that kills; the latter is a strength-giving and maturing realization. It is the key that opens the door to adulthood.

The authentic parent instills values into the life of his child now. But he also includes provisions for shedding these values. He gives his child *both* values *and* the freedom to reject these values at maturity. A set of values is like a life insurance policy. At maturity, it can be kept in force or cancelled for its cash value or annuity provisions.

The second overriding consideration in preventing Richard's kind of problem—the inability to cope with value-conflicts—is that the parent must have the proper distance from and perspective on his choices of values. The fearful parent is threatened by his freedom and imposes his religion or general value-system on his child, with no room for disagreement. The courageous and secure parent recognizes that his own values are his own choices, and he is prepared to assume full responsibility for his decisions and their consequences. Authentic parents share with their children the region of distance, relativity, and freedom in their commitment to values. The parent has the authority to rule that his values be his child's values, but the authentic parent recognizes and shares the game quality, the relativity, and the eventual flexibility which these philosophical realities imply. In the process, parent and child establish a deeper, a transcendental, union. They recognize that their true meeting ground is their common consciousness rather than their common value heritage or tradition. A dual, albeit dialectical, relation ensues. The two individuals are in two relations to each other: parent-child and friend-friend. There will be conflict between these distinct roles, but such contrast is merely a healthy expression of the needed bipolarity of consciousness itself (theme C 14 of the master table).

THE BODY IS A LIMIT

Another set of limits for which the authentic parent's lack of responsibility is communicated to the child are those which stem from the needs of the body. These limits lead to health rules, and parents are often confronted with the problem of how to enforce them. Frequently, health rules lead to a struggle between the will of the parent and that of the child. Such a confrontation of power is precisely what the authentic parent can avoid once he is aware of his exact level of responsibility.

In truth, it is not the parent who tells the child to brush his teeth or to keep regular bed time hours; it is the child's bodily nature; it is his biological essence. In the last analysis, it is the child's body and not the parent which says to the child, "Brush your teeth; go to bed." Perhaps the parent is the speaker or amplifier of the radio receiver that is the child's body, but it is the child who is speaking. When an argument over rational health rules develops, we have the ridiculous situation in which the receiver yells at the speaker for changing its electric impulses into audible airwaves or sound. When on top of that the parent feels responsible and guilty for insisting that his child observe a health rule, then the parent has totally forgotten that he but amplifies the sounds of the child's body, that the child is talking, not the parent. And through his inauthentic guilt, the parent promptly teaches this ignorance to his child as well. This ignorant misconception must be corrected in order to establish a program for authentic child raising. The parent must therefore learn to avoid assuming unwarranted responsibility. He is responsible for teaching the child that as parent he is *not* responsible for the validity of health rules.

For example, a mother should send this message: "It is your body that demands you brush your teeth, not your Mother, so don't tell me I'm compulsive about oral hygiene!" It is not the parent who tortures the child by insisting he take his medicine; it is the needs of his body that make this demand on *both* child *and* parent. Life is greatly simplified when the burden of unnecessary responsibility is lifted. This liberating attitude, although obvious, is often and incredibly overlooked.

Education—both its presence and its lack—is a still further limit. An educated person is limited by the needs that have sprouted and the expectations that have been born through a widening of horizons. An uneducated person is often at a disadvantage in the competition of the marketplace. He is subject to unnecessary fears and may be ignorant of where to search for answers to his questions. If he now also feels guilty and inadequate, he unnecessarily assumes personal responsibility for these limits. That guilt, which is neurotic, is paralyzing. The individual who recognizes in his lack of education a limiting fact for which he is not responsible will then also have the energy and ensuing freedom of action to do something constructive and rational to solve his problem.

HUMAN NATURE IS A LIMIT

In a deeper sense each person is further limited by the nature of man. Man is limited by the characteristics of his philosophical and transcendental nature (that is, the structure of his consciousness), and he is limited by external empirical reality (that is, the functions of his body, society, and the world of nature). Even man's absolute freedom of cathexis (identification) and constitution (the ascription of meaning) is a limit, in that man cannot free himself from this burden. Thus, in the last analysis, man's freedom is a limit, contradictory as this position might at first appear. Sartre was right when he said that man is condemned to be free.

One can go over each item of the master table and find in it not only a liberating insight into man's potential but also a corresponding and painful limit. In connection with each theme, you must say to yourself "I am not responsible for the existence of this limit, but I am responsible for coping with it!" For example, pain, death, and contradiction (anxiety), finitude, and polarity are certainly philosophical limits par excellence.

The same is true also of theme C 8 (Life), for instance. To say "yes" to life is a responsibility and often is not easy, especially when the logic of frustration, despair, and depression might tempt us and convince us otherwise. Love (theme C 10), beautiful as it is, is nevertheless bought at the price of losing independence and irresponsibility. Growth (theme C 13) is a distinct limit to him who is tired, who is exhausted by living and confronting and meeting. The field theory (theme A 1) is itself a limit. It forces ambiguity on man; it does not clearly either isolate or connect him with the world. Many persons are inauthentic because they refuse to accept the ambiguity of the field of consciousness as a bona fide limit. In other words, the nature of man, his philosophical essence, is possibly the most fundamental and most far-reaching limitation of our human existence.

The authentic parent knows that, accepts it, and does not blame himself for it. And he transmits that knowledge to his children through example, word, and deed. The benefit to the child is a better relation with his parents—he loves rather than condemns them—and an excellent model of adulthood—he is free of the weight of needless guilt.

Remember

1. Make clear to yourself and to others your absolute limits.
2. As a universal rule, you as parent are not responsible for the unalterable limits that life and the world impose upon you.
3. Do not accept blame for your limitations.
4. You must educate your children to understand the unalterable limits that surround them like impenetrable barriers.
5. You as a parent must not assume personal responsibility for those existential factors that realistically limit your child's life. You would then prevent him from learning the philosophical meaning of limits in his life.
6. Each child lives within the limits imposed upon him by the inauthentic character traits of his parents.
7. Your child is limited by the limitations of his parents.
8. A child must be told not to hold himself responsible for the kind of family into which he is born.
9. Each man is limited by the nature of human existence.
10. Each parent, even if he were perfect, is still limited by the philosophical nature of man, because
11. Even a parent's inescapable freedom or free will is a limit for him and for his children.
12. Each man is limited by the nature of his physical environment.
13. Physical nature limits both parents and children. And we, as parents or children, are not responsible for these limits. Furthermore,
14. The parent is not responsible for the limits society sets on the freedom of his children.
15. Inevitable injustice is a limit into life.
16. A child must be made aware of those economic conditions and circumstances of fate that limit his opportunities. His clear perception of these and his honest confrontation of them will give the child the strength of character to conquer the worst.
17. The needs of your body are absolute limits.
18. The body (including age) of the parent as well as that of the child is an unalterable limit that must and can be successfully confronted.
19. You as a parent need not change your individual values; you must help your child recognize that whereas these are indeed *your* firm values that they are *not* in themselves absolute nor universal.
20. Do not fear to guide your children strongly in the choice of values.
21. If you as parent make courageous commitments, you teach your child likewise to make courageous commitments. Do not teach him to imitate your choices, only the power of your commitment.
22. Be both close to and distant from your values.

23. The philosophical nature of man is a liberating blessing but also a series of limits. For example, "growth leads to meaning" is a fact that cannot be altered.

24. Here is a summary of authentic religious education:
    a. An authentic person makes decisions.
    b. Your freedom is my limit.
    c. Values are real.

18
Existential Parenthood
Know Your Freedom

We are now ready to discuss the final set of philosophical characteristics of man and to show how these influence authentic child-rearing. The focus here will be on existential freedom.

8. Each family has the right to be different

Be confident and secure in the definitions you have adopted or in the changes of self-definitions that you are in the process of making. Be assured that your definition of yourself, your marriage, the type of parent you are, and the concept of man expressed in your lifestyle are acceptable. We live in an age that demands that each of us must choose for himself. It is no longer possible to choose agreement with the "common values of society," because these no longer exist. The choice for conformism in our pluralistic society with its speedy and far-reaching systems of communication is no longer an alternative. Since that is the case, we must learn how to choose with confidence our own values and our self-definitions. We must be rational, reflective, and thoughtful, and we must forever remember that the uncertainties of guilt, regret, and second thoughts are but proof of the fact that our glorious human freedom is in operation. You will never be sorry for the choices you make under these free conditions. Your lifestyle does not need to be constantly compared to extrinsic standards and then doubted.

A local newspaper runs a cartoon series titled "Supermother." It implies that the ideal mother is always "perfect"—perfection being defined in terms of meaningless and artificial standards, based perhaps on what makes a perfect machine, and never in terms of what is subjective, conscious, and human. Supermother is cheerful toward her husband after a day of primitive struggles and gargantuan labors with the children and their problems. Supermother is patient with all the children even after a series of tantrums and catastrophes: The children are all in the bathtub together, enjoying a calamitous fight, which leaves the bathroom and its immediate environs utterly destroyed. In general, her children are creating bedlam while Supermother is cooking a sumptuous, elegant dinner for Daddy and his boss. Her solution—according to the professional advice of the cartoon's philosopher, the advertiser—is to take a widely marketed aspirin preparation, so that the "headache" this chaos gives her will disappear and she will again be able to play the role of the polished, proper, and patient multifaceted homemaker, or Supermother.

After the sedative has taken effect, Supermother handles the bathroom crisis rationally and kindly, possibly as Jesus might have, or perhaps Saint Teresa of Avila. Supermother, in truth, descends to the level of her children, becomes one of them, and identifies with the manic-hysterical and overstimulated humor in it all. In fact, she may even participate in the bedlam because, after all, a child is always right in our youth-oriented culture. And the effect of such a newspaper series is to make every gullible mother feel guilty and inadequate—a failure.

The authentic mother, on the other hand, may explode and send everyone to bed without supper and tell Daddy the evening with the boss is off: She can't handle the chaos! What's wrong with that? The exploding mother is simply expressing faith in her own choice of values. She is expressing the authenticity of her self-definition. She is testifying to the fact that she confidently accepts her needs and her limitations. Supermother gives us no such evidence. On the contrary, she demonstrates through her slavish behavior that she rejects completely any limits in herself. She feels guilty because she is not God. Supermother has not yet defined herself as human; she is still in the puerile stage of life when consciousness defines itself as infinite and as God. The authentic mother, in this case the explosive one, is authentic because she lives the insight that she is not to be guided by the current fads in motherhood nor is she defined by vacuous and accidental external standards. She is authentic because she has accepted her finitude and because she acts on that finitude. Supermother is inauthentic because she demands the impossible of herself: she refuses to accept the reality of her philosophical limits.

9. The locus of freedom shifts

Because of inevitable conflicts between children and parents we are led to the question, "Where in the social unit is the existential freedom

—the locus of all authentic actions—located?" In order to answer that question, I will make the assumption that there is only a fixed amount of freedom to be divided up among the various components of the single social unit that is the parent-child relationship. For example, in a permissive parent-child relationship, the freedom of the social unit is centered almost exclusively in the child. The indulgent parent assumes that the only freedom that exists or counts is that of his child. The child then grows up spoiled, with no realistic sense of objective limits. He grows up with a distorted and eventually undemocratic sense of the actual distribution of freedom in social units. On the other hand, in an authoritarian parent-child relation, the freedom in the social unit resides almost exclusively in the parent. That is an equally unbalanced assignment of freedom. What, then, is an authentic distribution?

Given a constant amount of the "substance" of freedom to be distributed between parent and child (that is, of course, a metaphor akin to the Freudian notion of libido), then the following situation obtains: At the birth of the child, all available freedom resides in the parent. The parent begins the life of the infant by defining him: He chooses for his child how to eat, when to sleep, and how to manage the social subtleties of defecation. Gradually, as the child is socialized, other values, roles and definitions are transmitted to him—or imposed on him without consultation; most of these, although their origin is in external society, are nevertheless filtered through and pumped by the free will of the parent.

What is the meaning of growing up, or maturing, for a child seen from this philosophical perspective? For the child to grow up, at any age, means for *the locus of freedom to shift.* Freedom is transferred from parent to child. That transfer is the existential-philosophical interpretation of growing up. As the child acquires more freedom, the parent loses an equivalent amount. The correlative draining and filling of freedom are traumatic experiences. Growth is always traumatic because the changes it involves are genuinely creative, and thus unexpected. No one can be prepared to receive or give, that is, to participate in, real creation and growth. Growing up as the transfusion of freedom is comparable to a direct blood transfusion from donor to recipient. It is a traumatic experience for both!

This analysis of parent-child interaction proves itself to be a particularly useful model in cases of the acerbic conflicts that often occur during the tumultuous teenage years. Here is an illustrative interchange, translated, of course, from the emotional and specific vernacular into its philosophical equivalences:

TEENAGER: Dad, you don't give me enough freedom. You are authoritarian.

FATHER: Don't fret. I should be the one to complain. With each minute of life, your freedom increases and mine decreases. You can look forward to endless freedom and I to none. Be patient; the future is yours. You are receiving my blood while I am losing it. My life flows into yours: You increase and I decrease in life. I am the fertilized soil from which you draw the nutriment to become a mature tree. The soil is thereby made sterile. The tree does not thank the soil; you need not thank me. But neither does the tree ask the soil to change its nature.

QUANTITIES OF FREEDOM

Who is to assign amounts of freedom? And what constitutes the "right" distribution? Between parent and child there is jockeying for position. There is constant mutual testing. In terms of ideal rules, one can argue that the child should have exactly as much freedom as he can handle. In any transfusion there is the proper and fit amount of blood. Too much is equally harmful as not enough. And how do we know the relative values, the proportionate amounts? This is a decision which can be made legally and sociologically in broadest outlines only—and in specific cases one depends on the judgment of an authentic individual who also happens to be a parent. No machine, no technique, and no test can substitute for the mature and subjective judgment of an authentic individual. Such an individual is sensitive to the existence of freedom within himself and both observant of and responsive to the workings of that freedom in his child. He observes daily the effects of the transfer and adjusts the dosage, as it were, accordingly.

This illustrates once more that the first requirement for being an authentic parent is to be an authentic person. No rules or techniques can substitute for artistry and experience in this crucial transfer of free will. Being a parent is an art and not a science. Our society's first concern must be with art, and not with science. The test for the degree of parental authenticity is to be found in the severity of the struggle for independence manifested by the teenager. If the struggle is bitter, the parent has probably been inauthentic in assigning the distribution of freedom, and he should seek immediate help or examine the situation himself from the point of view of freedom. Behavior problems at all ages can be constructively interpreted as symptoms of the inequitable distribution of freedom, too much or too little in parent or child.

For example, the spoiled and inconsiderate child, the whining and tantruming youngster, the contemptuous child, the child that has little relation with and respect for his parent may have more freedom than he can handle. The parent of this child has lost much of the freedom which, he now discovers, is needed for the proper upbringing of his offspring. He has forfeited his freedom by prematurely transferring it to the child.

Schoolwork, health habits, a sane life for the other members of the household, all of these facets of family life become intolerably difficult or they are completely disrupted because of an inauthentic distribution of freedom.

A common plant-killer is based on the principle that excessive hormones result in growth to the bursting point. The plant has "too much" health and potential; it has inadequate limits. As a result, it dies. The same has happened to the child in our example. He has been given more freedom, more human growth, maturity, and authenticity, than his frail, young body can handle. The resulting chaos is the destruction of the family world. Freedom without limits is as self-destructive and undesirable as limits without freedom.

On the other hand, the child who develops symptoms such as kleptomania or vandalism, who is truant or runs away from home, bullies and hurts others, or calls attention to himself in *indirect* ways is probably one in whose life freedom was withheld. Too much freedom was retained by parents, and the child's growth was stunted by a freedom-insufficiency.

The symptoms tell us about the authenticity and wisdom of the distribution of freedom; the symptoms are an index of the relative allotment of free will. The remedy is to be found in reassessing the freedom-distribution and in finding wise ways of administering this redistribution.

Morris and Karl

Let us examine the examples of Morris and Karl. Both are fourteen and freshmen in high school. Both have as their principal or most visible symptom poor school performance. Both are bright; neither makes any serious effort to succeed in school. Morris is a warm and affectionate personality. He relates well to teachers and other adults. He is polite and well liked. His gaze is direct. Karl, on the other hand, has a sly gaze. He does not relate well to adults; he spends little time at home and frequently expresses extreme derision for his parents. The guess of the school counselor was that the parent-child distribution of freedom was faulty in each case. This distribution was unwise and injudicious. Morris expresses symptoms of excessive freedom. His failure at school would then be due to his lack of self-discipline. He is an indulged child. He sees no need to do what he does not feel like doing.

Karl, however, shows signs of withheld freedom. He is cold and indifferent, aloof and "cool." Karl seems alone with his thoughts or fantasies most of the time. He can be cruel and thoughtless, something that does not appear in the behavior of Morris. Karl does not respond well to the kindness and interest extended to him by his teachers. His failure at school seems to be a form of anger, frustration, and rebellion. By failing himself and thereby also failing his parents, he is indirectly pressing against the barriers of his incarcerated self-transcendence. Freedom withheld becomes explosive frustration. Karl's home situation probably reflects a deprivation of free will. A simple interview proved the accuracy of both predictions regarding the relative allotment of freedom.

What remedies can an existential philosophy of man suggest? The first rule is to find a willing subjectivity with whom one can work. Is it to be that of the youngster or that of the parent? Ideally, both subjectivities should be enlisted, but this is often not possible. Let us consider proposed remedies from the point of view of the teenager primarily.

Morris's problem is how to give back some freedom to his parents, a prescription against which any teenager will rebel. Karl's problem is how to acquire more freedom, a recommendation that should please the average youngster. It is already apparent that the counselor will have an easier time enlisting Karl's co-operation rather than Morris's. This fact may appear paradoxical, since Morris is more affable than Karl and therefore he has a better relationship with the counselor.

A corollary of that paradox is reflected in the counselor's relation with the parents. While Morris is unapproachable on this point, his parents are receptive. They will gladly place more rigorous restrictions and limits on Morris. On the other hand, to the degree that Karl is receptive, his parents are not. These changes of freedom-distribution are likely to require major personality transformations in the parents, something that usually is beyond the scope of the average high school counselor. Nevertheless several specific steps can be recommended:

(1) The counselor should verbalize the situation explicitly. That is to say, he should *explain* to Morris that (a) his parents have given him more freedom than a boy his age can handle, and (b) that he should, in turn, explain that to his parents (or the counselor should). In most cases resistances and angry rebuttals arise immediately, and from *both* generations. The message for Karl is (a) his parents have not given him enough freedom for his age, and (b) he should tell this to his parents (or the counselor can).

(2) The next step in this rational and intellectual existential analysis of the problem is to point out that the problem is not with the adolescents themselves but it exists at home. The boys must be informed that the environment can be changed at home and at school to better suit their needs. This attitude is not an illegitimate shifting of responsibility; it simply calls attention to the fact that at age fourteen decisions regarding parent-child distribution of free will rest with the parent, not with the adolescents or the school. Some young teenagers are old enough to at least understand that point.

In this connection, Karl is better off than Morris. Karl can increase his freedom through the extreme gesture of running away. Needless to say, that solution brings with it other difficulties, but the world offers room to him who must increase his freedom. The same is not true of Morris. He cannot force the world to increase his limits, to diminish his freedom. He can only limit his freedom himself, but that is *not* the same as forcing the world to give him less freedom. In other words, Morris needs to be more mature than Karl to resolve his problem.

On the surface a parent may think that spoiling is better than strictness if he must choose among two evils in child-rearing. The present analysis, however, suggests the opposite: It is easier for a youngster to fight the evils of strictness than of spoiling. There is a corollary for the parent: Parents who spoil are easier to reach with requests for stricter child-raising than are authoritarian parents with the corresponding requests to become more permissive. Not being thought rigid enough is rarely interpreted by the parents as criticism, whereas being called too strict often is a threatening confrontation. There are, in turn, reasons also for these responses to the threat areas. Permissive parents have an "open" personality structure. They will therefore also be open to a teacher's or a counselor's suggestion or criticism. Strict parents, on the other hand, will tend to be "closed" to all, including school counselors with recommendations.

Since the school cannot take over the boys' home life, the school must investigate its own options. Morris's teachers can make increased demands on him and withdraw privileges to give him the experience of limits. Karl, however, should be permitted to choose his courses with greater freedom and what they will cover, his extracurricular activities, etc. He needs fewer rather than more limits. Both boys will respond well to such manipulation of their boundaries.

REMEMBER

1. Trust your values.
2. Parents need not always be rational, understanding, and kind. They, like children, also have emotional limits.
3. Growing up means that the freedom of the parent is transferred to his child.
4. Freedom without limits is as destructive as limits without freedom.
5. Have faith in your ability to make choices.
6. Parent and child have a finite amount of freedom to distribute between them.
7. The spoiled child has too much freedom.
8. The child with symptoms (such as problems with school) does not have sufficient freedom.
9. It is easier for a child to cope with excessive strictness than with excessive permissiveness.

10. Expect your child to grow up authentic, but allow him to choose how to express that authenticity.

11. You can establish a transcendental relation with your child, especially as he leaves home.

12. You have only one irrevocable commitment in life—a commitment to your child.

19
Linda's Marriage

Linda wrote me the following letter for discussion in a small summer workshop.

One of my main purposes for enrolling in this workshop was that I might better be able to face and organize the facts of my troublesome marriage relationship. Perhaps the most difficult aspect of the situation for me is to distinguish between fact and illusion.

The relationship has been noticeably deteriorating over the last two years, in particular.

I studied with you before. After your lectures, I began completely to change my view of myself: from being self-denying and confused, trying to please everyone but myself, trying to act out the role which I perceived society to have imposed upon me, I began to see myself as an individual with needs, and especially choices that would define me in different terms than simply wife and mother.

This process taking place within me has definitely altered my relationship with my husband. This relationship was once mainly quite pleasant but underneath an uneasiness was always vaguely perceptible. When I finished my BA—in art— ten years ago I felt that my art and my life were empty and meaningless. I felt this to be so because I had no close relationships, no family of my own. So marriage and four children ensued. As stated, the relationship was always pleasant but my feeling was that after I took care of this, the human side of my life, I would have purpose and be able to communicate that in my art. So always I had the uneasiness and guilt feelings involved with getting back to my art training. Now I have been back in school for a year, and I have been accepted

156

to the art graduate program. I feel like I am gathering momentum all the time and am truly ready to face and explore this part of me.

Now—how this affects the relationship. During this time my husband has suffered several job layoffs. Strictly the industry—nothing in relation to him. Nonetheless it has been difficult and troublesome to him and financially extremely difficult.

We have been finding that our relationship seems out of gear; when we face and encounter one another there is always conflict which seems so damaging and nonproductive.

Concerning the manner in which we relate—it is extremely difficult for me to be completely open with him because when I expose my real and vulnerable feelings to him, he uses that information to scold or exert authority over me. My response has been to withdraw from him and entrench myself more deeply into my art work. He is then the more enraged and attempts a further withdrawal from me in retaliation. In communication, the intimate closeness, the emotional touching of another which I seek seems to be too painful an experience or area for him. He seems to prefer a greater psychological distance or a more surface type of relationship than I do. All of these factors seem to indicate separation/ divorce.

Yet I cannot seem to reconcile myself to this idea or action. I have been caught in the grip of trying to deal with this decision for many months now. Neither of us seems to be able to take any action on it. I feel betrayed by our first dreams of what our family life would be. I can't seem to give up that ideal in my head of a wholesome family life for our children (boy 9/girl 7½/girl 6/boy 4). It seems infuriating that we can't create this atmosphere that we seek. I want a divorce. But I'm afraid.

The work load for me seems so staggering then that I feel loath to embark upon it again because (1) it will mean even less time with my children and (2) I am afraid that it will curtail and damage the momentum and progress I am making in my art work (which at this time represents the fragility of my being—everything I am). Yet if we stay in this relationship it is not enhancing to either of us personally and seems to be more destructive than anything else. For my part I sometimes feel that I am destroyed either way.

My husband sometimes suggest that I leave the family and then I could work only to support myself and go to school. I cannot accept this image of myself as one who could leave her children. He then states that he doesn't want to leave or be without his children either, which puts me in the position of feeling that I have no right to ask him to leave any more than he does me.

The dynamics between us has become so fraught with hostilities and resentments that it seems impossible for anything positive to again take place. The thought that there must be something else I can do frequently haunts me. Yet I know within that this is not so; I cannot go back to denying myself—not facing and finding what I am. I want a divorce but haven't got the strength to carry it through.

Following are some existential comments on Linda's problem.

She seeks help. What can she expect from counseling? In fact, what is the goal of therapy, philosophic or otherwise? Is it to help her achieve certain goals that are set *before* therapy and *before* philosophy and are thus psychologically and philosophically naïve and unexamined? Or is a therapeutically oriented philosophy a scrutiny of these very goals themselves? Is the role of therapeutic philosophy to make a marriage work, or is it to help the individual to disclose himself to himself, regardless of consequences? These questions must be asked before an existentially oriented philosophic therapy can help Linda.

Theoretical as well as practical difficulties result from such questions. On the theoretical level, it is an insight of the utmost importance to recognize that if philosophic therapy is the examination of the goals of life then there can be no way to evaluate and measure the effectiveness of therapy. Effectiveness is measured against a goal. Philosophic therapy has no goal in that sense. If there is a measure, it is whether or not the individual is learning something.

On the practical level, Linda must ultimately decide whether she desires a goal-oriented (symptom-removal) approach to the examination of what troubles her or a knowledge-oriented (self-disclosing) approach. These two directions represent entirely different purposes. The first direction has for its purpose to allay the symptom—to take a couple of aspirin tablets as an anodyne for a toothache. The second direction has for its purpose to get to the cause—the dentist pulls the abscessed tooth. The second direction lays bare the structure of human nature: Self-knowledge becomes an intrinsic value, an end in itself. That is philosophic therapy.

The only ethical way to handle the conflict between symptom-removal and philosophical understanding of human existence (a saved marriage or successful self-disclosure in this case) is to confront Linda early with the reality of the choice. Does she wish to be manipulated into a marriage that she can live with, that will not be particularly troublesome, and that will provide a secure basis for the children's growth, with the attendant possibility that her own innermost nature will be neither recognized nor met, will neither be understood nor expressed? Or does she want to take her chances at facing her philosophical nature, with all its troublesome freedom, its uncertainty, its risk, and its great emptiness?

Linda's Options

If she makes the latter choice and succeeds in achieving significant intellectual and emotional philosophic self-disclosure, then she will be confronted with various options for reorganizing her life. All these options are predicated on the existential premise, introduced at the beginning of this book, that *love, sex, marriage, and family are independent variables.* They are independent of each other, and *they are also inde-*

pendent of the quest for meaning and self-disclosure. Whatever connection or severance an actual life displays is *chosen,* with full responsibility on the part of the chooser.

On one hand, this insight is a grave and weighty burden requiring cosmic decisions. On the other, however, it is a great unburdening liberator of mankind. It spells the end of slavery to social norms and artificial values. It is the end of man being someone other than and external to himself. It is the beginning of man being himself.

Linda's options include the following:

(1) She can rechoose her marriage and make the most of an unsatisfactory and difficult situation, principally for the sake of the children. This choice is different from the adaptation to marriage suggested before because now she is self-disclosed, and from within that self-disclosure she freely chooses to limit her marital possibilities. This choice is what, in the general principles of marital adjustment, can be called "finding meaning in life *in spite* of marriage."

(2) She can file for divorce, and she can do it with either of two thoughts in mind: never to remarry or to remarry eventually. If she chooses never to remarry, it is because her self-disclosure has revealed to her that she will be most fulfilled, and a better mother, if she does not burden her life with a marriage. She recognizes that marriage is neither "natural" nor "unnatural" but chosen as a lifestyle and a means for self-fulfillment. She will have chosen "finding meaning in life *without* marriage" as her lifestyle. But if she chooses to remarry—or if she at least hopes for it and plans on it—she has decided to find her fulfillment *in* marriage and *with* marriage. She will then have chosen to leave her present marriage and re-establish another one on more mature grounds, something she is confident will succeed because of her increased self-disclosure.

(3) Linda can go one step further and seek a marriage that will be *more* than a success. A merely "successful" marriage represents one of several equal values in life: Profession, friends, travel, and the like are perceived as values of equivalent worth. That is what is meant by finding meaning in life *with* marriage as an adjunct. But a marriage that is more than a success is one based on the principle of finding meaning in life *through* marriage. The marriage then becomes an existential marriage, that is to say, one that is a metaphor for the structure of existence itself. Marriage then becomes the totality of the meaning of life for the couple. In an existential marriage the risk is total, since the individual acquisition of meaning is made wholly dependent on the richness and authenticity of the marriage relationship. If the marriage fails, being itself has vanished in the night.

(4) A fourth option that the decision for self-disclosure will open up

for Linda is to work on her present marriage. She will endeavor to reform her marriage. The following existential steps are required: First, she must choose the relation between meaning and marriage. Is it to be *without, in spite of, with* or *through* marriage that she will seek meaning? Second, she must choose to use the raw materials given to her—her present, actual marriage. Finally, she must choose to risk the hard work, serious commitment, and courageous stands required to attempt such a dramatic conversion of her present marriage.

Linda will then have chosen in effect not to put up with it and adjust to her present marriage—which was the first choice—but to be the marriage's therapist. That decision presupposes the greatest strength and maturity of all those discussed. It may be Linda's preferred decision, but is she aware of its enormous difficulty? Of all the options it is the easiest to choose but the most difficult to carry out.

IMPLEMENTATION

Once Linda has gone through the three existential steps needed for her resolve to change her present troubled marriage into an authentic one (define the meaning of her marriage, decide to build on what she already has, and choose to be strong), then she must further understand that to *implement* this option involves two separate subchoices. First, to save the marriage implies Linda's resolution to improve it, which is the decision not to accept its present status. If Linda approaches her husband with that kind of a resolve, and at the same time makes clear to him she means it, he will be either profoundly threatened, vastly relieved, or both. Any woman's determination is a potentially explosive confrontation, since her husband's masculine role is put in question; in fact, it is assaulted and his lifestyle, the status quo, is undermined.

Linda can present her firm resolve for an authentic marriage to her husband in various ways, none of which may please him. And they might not even work. Nevertheless, she has chosen to be determined and she is going to take risks accordingly. One way in which any woman can confront her husband with her determination to improve the marriage is to insist on joint counseling—either marriage or family therapy. Another is to do it herself, by simply announcing what she expects of the marriage and then helping her husband bring it about. A third alternative in communication is to draw up a written contract, perhaps even a witnessed one, with the help of the family lawyer in extreme cases. In it the woman's demands on the marriage will be stated explicitly: She will put in writing what she is prepared to do and what she expects from her husband. And the legal witness to the contract provided by the presence of the lawyer will underscore the seriousness of her commitment: She has made a grave promise to herself and to her husband.

DETERMINATION

The fulcrum on which the resolve is balanced is the woman's determination, which is a combination of understanding and willpower. To make a decision is to be resolute, to have made up one's mind, to cease wavering, and to mean business. This seriousness is the crucial point, and it cannot rest on willpower alone. It must also be real. Willpower is an external imposition on consciousness. The will, in the act of willpower, is experienced as external to the center. Willpower is the objective dimension of the phenomenon of resoluteness. Understanding is the subjective aspect of resoluteness. Understanding is that aspect of resoluteness which comes from the inside and moves out towards the world. It makes resoluteness natural, easy, and graceful.

If you are married, think of your own marriage and reflect on how these existential ideas can be of help to you. Are you "serious" about developing a good marriage? In all real decisions (decisions which "mean business") the inward, subjective pole is the *positive* pole. It is the pole from which growth emanates; it is the creative and spontaneous, the expressive aspect of the total phenomenon of resoluteness or resolve. The outward, object pole of consciousness is the *negative* pole of the phenomenon of resoluteness. That is the self-discipline of willpower.

An individual who is pure positive self-expression is as destroyed as one who is pure negative restriction. The former is a bum and the latter, a zombie. The individual who feels alive and a participant in the world (a true being-in-the-world) is a positive subjectivity that has chosen a certain amount of objective negativity. The subjective tendency for total self-indulgence is tempered by the objective tendency for total and repressive mechanization. *The experience of spontaneously and creatively choosing limits and structure is the unique experience of being human, healthy, and authentic.*

The resolve to improve a marriage, like any act of resoluteness and decisiveness, is the experience of an interface between consciousness and object, mind and matter. A choice is not a decision until the conscious thought of it is translated into irretrievable action. The thought is not a decision, even though it may be generated spontaneously, until this form of pure consciousness is translated into worldly waves. The choice occurs at the precise boundary between subject and object, consciousness and world, that is, the intentional and dialectical ambiguity of human existence. Linda's resolve to transform her impossible marriage into an authentic one must be conveyed unambiguously to her husband in addition to being obvious to herself. An iron resolve is thus the first requirement of Linda's choice to improve her marriage. And that is based heavily on a subjective and philosophical self-disclosure and not exclusively on a mechanical faith in willpower.

BE YOUR OWN MARRIAGE THERAPIST

A second major aspect of Linda's decision to improve the marriage is the implication that she will unfailingly and patiently, like a single-minded therapist, *work* for the improvement of the marriage. She will be demanding only as far as she knows her husband can tolerate it. She will understand his needs, his problems, and his strengths, and she will work with them intelligently and compassionately. She will make her own needs subservient to the needs of the marriage. She will develop infinite patience, since a transformed marriage is her goal. She will find her meaning in life, at least temporarily, not in an authentic marriage but in the *quest* for an authentic marriage. She will be rational in that she will recognize everyone's psychological limits to stress. She will identify zones of stress—even the plain physical stress of overwork—and avoid these or at least neutralize them when possible because she understands how severely the needs of the body limit human beings.

No guarantees can be offered to Linda, but it is likely that if she can sustain such a rational strategy—perhaps with some additional external therapeutic support—for a long time, hopeful if not dramatic changes will gradually begin to appear in her marriage. Should her marriage collapse after all, the growth experienced by Linda will alone have been worth the price.

LINDA'S RESPONSIBILITY

Linda, for her own sake, needs a lesson in the philosophical description of responsibility. We all need to remember that in the existential view responsibility is a *fact* of human nature and not just moralistic Victorian double-talk. If you understand *that* you are responsible, then you will find it possible to *act* responsibly.

Like you, Linda is a freedom, and as such she, like you, creates. She is the godlike creator of her life (theme A 3, responsibility, of the master table). She is the architect of the world in which she exists. But beyond that she is also its builder and its construction workers. A highly developed sense of responsibility is but her realization that she is the agent of these superstructures of her life. If you wish to know how mature you really are, remember this: Nothing discloses your maturity more readily than a highly developed sense of responsibility. You are an authentic individual if you understand the connection between your free choices and the reality which they create.

Take Sally, for instance. She is twenty-four, has two children, and is in the process of finalizing a divorce from her husband, Todd. She is having an affair with George, who is unmarried but, as an incensed Sally will find out later, is also quite a philanderer. Sally signed up for one of my couples' workshops *and paid also for George.* The group is strictly limited and the demand for places is high, so that each place occupied excludes another interested member. After only one meeting, George left for another city and another woman. Sally wants me to refund her the fee she paid for George. What is the most authentic way for me to handle the refund question? How can I use her request to help her understand the existential meaning of responsibility?

Let us examine this small episode with Sally in the light of the meaning of responsibility so as to help Linda understand what responsibility means in her life. Both Sally and George had built up a self-indulgent, neurotic, puerile, and irresponsible social structure. Sally paid for George, hoping to manipulate herself and him into what she hoped would be marital compatibility. That is inauthenticity number one. Manipulation is the result of a ghost-in-a-machine theory of man and cannot lead to authentic human relationships. Thus, Sally's paying for George was an objective worldly structure resting nevertheless on the foundation of a subjective free act. That free act, that choice, was irresponsible in that it did not conform to the flow of consciousness which is the nature of man. It was a choice based on the premise that people, including Sally herself, are things and that happiness is a particular shape or order of things.

Inauthenticity number two is George's acceptance of the arrangement. He *is* his choice. He therefore *is* a child, not a man. He does not take the direction of his life into his own hands; he lets Sally do it for him as if she were his mother. Hidden in that passivity with respect to life's basic values may also lurk George's hostility. What an elegant way to express anger and wreak vengeance on women!

Inauthenticity number three is George's inconsiderateness to the person excluded from the group by his presence. He occupied a place and then wasted it. In effect, he wasted someone else's place.

Finally, inauthenticity number four, is the request for return of the money. Sally expects the group's sponsor to redeem her for her own inauthenticity. She erred but expects someone else to pay. This is a key point, since it is evidence for Sally's (and George's) unwillingness to assume responsibility for her life. Sally's problem is diagnosed at this very point. Sally and George do not expect to accept their own actions as theirs; they do not understand that they are the architects of the structure that is their lifestyle. They have constructed a building, i.e., they have made a commitment, and the next minute they have forgotten or ignored that they made such a commitment.

We see in this relatively insignificant episode a larger philosophic truth that can reach into all aspects of your personal life: As a mature and authentic individual you *know* that the small and limited social world which you have constructed around yourself is of your own creation and is thus a part of yourself. Your world is an extension of your freedom. The moment that you, through words or actions, deny that continuity, you have become irresponsible. As soon as you reject the reality of the continuous field from free act to consequences; that is to say, as soon as you break up the unity of subject and object, you have split the universe, you have denied yourself, you have shown the most gross ignorance. You are then a person for whom negation has disappeared from your life. That is to say, you have excluded *reality* and *otherness* —that which is beyond your control and which is to be respected as different from you—from your personality structure. You will have become a person of pure expression but of no self-disclosure, hence, you are not real. You are now not mature but self-indulgent.

Responsibility, however, does not mean compulsiveness. A responsible individual creates a world for himself to which he can be devoted in good conscience. He makes only those commitments which are in harmony with the larger designs he has for his life. Responsible behavior is thus a key index to authenticity. And that is a lesson, a truth about human existence that Linda must learn.

If Linda opts to save the marriage, she needs a clear understanding of the meaning of existential responsibility illustrated by the Sally-George episode.

Linda's Meaning

Evidently art plays an important role in the resolution of Linda's marital problems. She has not come to terms with the problem of the meaning of life, which is the dual problem of how to contend with finitude and how to grow. Linda expects her marriage to do that job for her. In fact, however, she like all of us must do that job alone.

How can she do it? How can she lift the burden of meaning-creation from her marriage and place it where it belongs, in the zone of life which is exclusively hers? She can do it through her art. Each person must find his own creative endeavor. Painting, like all expressions of art, has as its specific aesthetic function the task of wrestling with the problem of searching for meaning in life. Art may be our finest language and sharpest tool in the quest for meaning. It is far better suited to grapple with the meaning of life, with death, meaninglessness, and freedom than is a mere marriage, a social institution based on tribal traditions.

Linda tells us that her art is empty. But what should be the subject-matter of her art? It is her despair about life, her anguish about life's lack of meaning. The emptiness itself must become the topic for her art. In fact, I would say that she should express artistically her *protest*—anger, despair, frustration—against the artlessness in her life and in her paintings. *Protest* is the key. Protest against death, against emptiness, against meaninglessness, against bad art, and against uninspired paintings. These are Linda's authentic philosophical feelings. These are the philosophical moods and insights that make her commitment to art a necessity for survival.

In sum, Linda's art must express—both as despair and as protest against that despair—her agony about life, about her marriage, about her meaning, about her womanhood, and about her many frustrations and her unfulfilled needs.

When Linda finally accomplishes this task of protest (in philosophy we call it emotive language) in her art she will have "expressed," stated, expelled for view not only something for herself: *She will have accomplished it for all mankind!* She is not engaged in an individual, personal, and unique task. She is doing the universal work of mankind. She is doing what all of us, regardless of the specific circumstances of our lives, are doing or should be doing.

All these considerations are good news for Linda. Her problem is mostly within her. Her problem is basically one of meaning. It is far easier for Linda to come to terms with the universal philosophical problem of finding meaning in life within herself than to change the personality of her husband and herself and to modify the institution of marriage. And the marvelous aspect of all this is that the real locus of the problem is in the inward search for meaning and not in the manipulation of her marriage. If she deals with the one issue that she can handle—the quest for meaning through art—its effects will reverberate throughout all the corridors of her life: her success in school, her professional success, and her success as mother, woman, daughter, and wife.

OUR PROBLEMS ARE UNIVERSAL

Her problem is definitely not a personal one but a universal, philosophical one. She is not sick but human. She, like Jesus, or any other important religious figure, is charged with the responsibility of solving the problem of the meaning of life (death against life, finitude against self-transcendence, God against man) for all of us. That is a noble task. That is the task of the artist. Her marriage, like her relations with all people, will find its proper place vis-à-vis this largest of life's tasks. What is true of Linda is also true of you in many of the troublesome aspects of your life.

It is unnecessary, even a mistake, to trace the origins of Linda's problem to childhood maladjustments, to relations to father and to mother, and to sexual difficulties. These may well be partial sources of the difficulties. They may form shadings in the total picture. But they are not the foundation—neither the canvas nor the inspiration, neither the form nor the content—of the painting that is to be Linda's life. Linda's principal source of agony is a universal philosophical issue. She attempts to work out philosophical issues in terms of their symbolic symptoms. That project is an escape. By blaming her marriage—or even her husband—for her sense of meaninglessness, she confesses that she demands from her marriage (which is an event external to her subjective inwardness and consciousness) the management of the problem of the meaning of life, the management of life's underlying anxiety. That transfer from philosophy to sociology, from herself to her marriage, is a decision for inauthenticity; it is a decision for being someone else; it is a decision for having another (person or institution) do her living for her. That is in effect a decision to avoid responsibility for being herself. It is a decision for philosophic ignorance. And that ignorance leads to painful symptoms in life, mostly a sense of ennui. In other words, the search for meaning is essentially a subjective task. And that is good news for Linda and for all of us, since now we realize that these problems can be managed, lived with, and solved.

But a final word is in order. Her deepest human relations including the one with her husband can exist with other persons engaged in a similar lonely and protesting search. Social institutions such as friendship, classes, discussion groups, therapy, and social gatherings of kindred minds make possible the meeting of minds on profound levels of empathy and understanding, without embarrassment and immorality.

I would like to conclude this analysis of Linda's marital troubles with excerpts from one of Linda's later letters:

Our marriage took place, to begin with, for neurotic, clinging, lonesome needs—you were right in that and absolutely correct in the observations that each of us then had huge expectations that the other was supposed to supply the meaning of life. Now, I certainly don't feel that way, and although my husband intellectualizes that he doesn't, all of his actions and attitudes towards me show that he's still furious with me for not being perfect. He is the perfect example of the hypothetical individual you spoke of who runs several miles a day, lifts weights, frets about what he eats, disparages himself about losing weight, organizes his finances and yet is about to go crazy trying to organize his head. His main frustration is that he has no goals and sees no meaning to his life. He seems to be one of those people who is the most comfortable when he is miserable. If you pay him a compliment, he will quickly tear himself down.

As to his feelings about me—he feels immensely threatened by my independence. He is extremely jealous over my other relationships—he imagines all sorts of wild things and relationships that most assuredly go on at school. If I'm late he thinks I've slept with the instructor.

I have been coming to feel that perhaps I fit your description of the inauthentic individual who deludes himself about his condition, seeks to escape responsibility for himself, etc., because I don't seem to be able to make any decisions or take any actions that would make life more pleasant and liveable.

I think a great deal of the problem is in my husband's feelings of inadequacy, meaninglessness, etc. Yet although he's always complaining about that, he refuses to commit himself to doing anything about it. I am, essentially, his scapegoat— the reason that the world is screwed up for him, etc. I haven't effectively been able to communicate that I will no longer be a scapegoat, because the unacceptable behavior and attitudes still keep coming my way.

I feel extremely confident that I will succeed with my life, following the suggestions you have made. I feel much encouraged; also determined and hopeful.

Five years later I saw both Linda and her husband for a brief period. They were changed people and seemed definitely on the way to joyously fulfilling their human potential.

REMEMBER

1. Love, sex, marriage, family, and meaning are independent variables.
2. A person can choose to find meaning in life *without* marriage.
3. A person can choose to find meaning in life *through* marriage.
4. A person can choose to find meaning in life *in spite of* marriage.
5. A person can choose to find meaning in life by *reforming* his or her marriage.
6. To be healthy is to spontaneously choose limits, to freely choose structure.
7. A sure sign of maturity is a developed sense of responsibility.
8. Do not burden your marriage by insisting it be the source of meaning in your life.
9. Protest is an authentic act.
10. The search for meaning is a subjective task.

APPENDIX A
The Master Table

The following master outline summarizes the insights about the nature of man and the character of his happiness developed by a hundred years of existential philosophy. The outline is carefully formulated to emphasize the practical application of existential philosophy.

A. THE NATURE OF HUMAN EXISTENCE

1. **The Field Theory of Man: "I am neither a body nor a soul but a continuous consciousness-body-world field." (Intentionality)**
(Explanation: I do not exist in isolation. I am one with other people and one with nature. Whatever affects other people and the environment also affects me and whatever happens to me affects other people and the world around me.)

2. **The Two Selves: "I am a pure consciousness that has a psychological personality, a physical body, and many social roles." (Transcendental and empirical egos)**
(Explanation: I am more than just a body and even more than a personality. I am also a pure consciousness or a pure awareness that is different from the person that is known by the name that I carry and the likeness that I am. I am a center, the depths of which only I can plumb.)

2a. **Five Modes of Consciousness: "Consciousness can be experienced as either individual, intimate, social, cosmic, or as an Eternal Now" (Transcendental intersubjectivity)**
(Explanation: I understand that there is much confusion about the nature of the ego, since different cultures have different definitions of what it means to be a self. I am capable and willing to experience and identify with at least four separate and increasingly deeper and more universal ways in which the consciousness that I am or that runs through me can manifest itself in me. The first, and most common, is the experience of consciousness as being an individual. Individual

169

consciousness is the silent and solitary center of all my experiences. Individual consciousness feels comfortable with itself but isolated from other people and from the world of nature.

I am also an intimate or intersubjective consciousness. I can experience complete oneness with another person. There exists a perceptible connecting conscious space between me and another person. I can perceive the center of another person directly; I can also sense how another experiences my center directly.

Third, I have social awareness and I achieve an identity through social groups.

Fourth, I can experience the fact that I am part of a cosmic conscious stream and that I share and participate fully in the endless processes of nature. I am a wave in an ocean of consciousness; I am a well, as all others are wells (to use Ira Progoff's metaphor), which taps into a single underground stream, together with all the other wells. I am coterminal with empty space-time.

A fifth, final, and the deepest level in which consciousness manifests itself is what can be called the Eternal Now. In it, even space-time becomes an object to consciousness. The Eternal Now as the source of consciousness is experienced to be outside of space and time. A psychic distance has been inserted between the ego as the Eternal Now and its most primitive objects, empty space and time.

3. Responsibility: "I have created and am responsible for the organization of my world. I did not create the raw materials, but I am fully and alone responsible for the social reality that I have constructed around me and the lifestyle that I have organized for myself." (Constitution)

(Explanation: If I am happy and successful, then it is essentially not fate and luck but my own efforts and decisions that have led to my well-being. If I fail and am unhappy, then I am prepared to assume full responsibility for my problems. I feel that my problems are basically my fault since I am in charge of my life—no one else is. It is good news to know that I help shape both the good and the bad in the world in which I live. I am prepared to fulfill my obligations.)

B. The Rule for a Meaningful Human Existence

1. Self-disclosure: "I must be fully disclosed to myself both as a human being and as _____ (write your name in this space)." (Phenomenology)

(Explanation: I am excited at the thought of both therapy and philosophy. I look forward to exploring the person that I am. I anticipate with pleasure examining my feelings and attitudes. I want to study my personality and my body. I am also determined to understand the philosophical nature of man. I recognize the importance of questions regarding human destiny and about the meaning of life. I also appreciate the significance of morality. I consider these questions fundamental to a free and healthy life.)

C. The Sixteen Principles for Authentic Human Existence

1. Pain: "I choose to value my pains." (Negation: Anxiety)

(Explanation: Suffering can be a learning experience. Pain is unavoidable. Death is a natural part of life. Anxiety and depression help me understand the meaning of life. I can successfully cope with the fact that evil is an integral part of life.)

2. Death: "I choose to value my limitations." (Negation: Finitude)

(Explanation: I can adapt myself to frustrations. I know that much of the time I cannot have what I want. I know that over a lifetime I will be forced to give up many of my most cherished dreams. I am successful in accepting that which cannot be helped. I can accept the fact that all life ends in death.)

3. **Reflection: "I am able both to *live* my life and to *reflect* on my life."** (Epoche, Reduction)

(Explanation: There are times at which I am active and extroverted. I participate in life and I am involved. There are also times at which I am withdrawn and reflective, that is, introverted. If I so choose, I can meditate and be happy just being by myself and inside myself. I have control over these feelings and attitudes. They are usually appropriate to the circumstances of my life.)

4. **Self-reliance: "I am an adult consciousness that exists alone: I choose to be independent and self-reliant."** (Inwardness, Subjectivity)

(Explanation: I have outgrown childish forms of dependency. I can be comfortable being alone. I can go through life on my own two feet. I can take care of myself—and of others if necessary. I feel that this independence and self-reliance is an attitude that I voluntarily choose and not one that is imposed upon me from the outside. This theme is in contrast to the later themes of commitment [9] and love [10]).

5. **Individuality: "It is right and normal for me to seem different from other human beings."** (Uniqueness)

(Explanation: I am free to conform or not to conform as my value system dictates. I am not excessively bothered by the fact that I may be different from my peers. I am prepared to create my own direction and my own life, one that I know is right for me even though it may differ from the prevailing lifestyles of those around me. I am not easily pressured by my associates and relatives. Neither am I easily pressured by my neighbors, by people that I meet or by those who try to sell me something.)

6. **Eternity: "There exists a consciousness within me which I am and which is eternal."** (Transcendental ego)

(Explanation: This point is perhaps the most difficult one to understand. It means that I have a genuine conception and perception of my most inner inwardness. I have a real sense of the center that I am within me amidst the storms, stresses and changes of life. I understand what sages of all ages mean when they refer to the pure consciousness within me that I am. I also recognize the universality of that center. The conscious center that I am is not susceptible to the flux of life and is therefore unchanging and timeless. It may not last forever, but it is outside of time.)

6a. **Reverence: "Each individual human inward subjectivity is the divine consciousness in man."** (Transcendental subjectivity)

(Explanation: Reverence for subjectivity is the highest existential principle of morality. A person's character may be evil and his body diseased, but his pure inner conscious core is infinitely precious and eternally dignified. Man's inwardness is the source of his value; his inmost center is the foundation for his "unalienable rights of life, liberty and the pursuit of happiness" with which each individual, according to the American Declaration of Independence, is born.

I am capable of respecting infinitely the inner ego of both myself and of others. I can "hate the sin rather than the sinner." I agree with Maritain when he says "the true connection among people is spiritual.")

7. Freedom: "I always choose because I am always free." (Freedom)

(Explanation: I have a realistic sense of the profound meaning of human freedom. I believe in the existence of free will. I believe that I am responsible for my actions and for my life. I believe that I set my own values and self-concepts and I am prepared to accept the full consequences. I am able to make decisions even while I realize that in most situations there are no definite truths and falsehoods, rights and wrongs.)

8. Life: "My first and last choice is to say 'yes' to life." (Affirmation)

(Explanation: If I say "yes" to life I recognize that I am fully responsible for whatever optimism or pessimism runs through my existence. If I am depressed *I* have said "no" to life. If I live with joy it is because *I* have said "yes" to life. If I say "yes" to life I freely choose to make living itself the highest value. In short, whether I love life or not, whether I am a positive or a negative personality is my own free personal choice for which I am fully responsible. I cannot blame others for my depression, anger, guilt or lack of self-respect.)

9. Commitment: "I am free to make commitments." (Commitment, Cathexis)

(Explanation: Commitment and love represent a contrast to the theme of self-reliance [4]. Commitment means that I feel connected with the world: I feel one with my body and one with the society and environment into which as a human being I am born. Commitment means that I can risk attachments to people, principles, goals, and life styles. I can take it if I lose. Commitment means that I can live as a full-fledged participant in the affairs of society and of the natural environment. My life is experienced whole rather than fragmented.)

9a. Reality: "I clearly distinguish reality from fantasies, dreams, rationalizations and wishful thinking. I am always in touch with what is real." (Ego-cogito-cogitatum)

(Explanation: I have a well-developed sense of reality. Even though I understand that the distinction between dream and reality is philosophically ambiguous, I find no difficulty separating dream from reality in my daily and practical life. I know that there is a reality beyond my inwardness. I know that this reality is different from my subjective ego. I know that this reality may be other people or the objects of nature, but it can also be my body or my unconscious [as I see in cases of physical or mental illness]. I know that this reality is independent of me: sometimes it joins me in my needs and wishes, sometimes it is indifferent and sometimes it opposes me. Nevertheless, at all times I feel that I am directly in touch with that external reality. I always sense that I am in contact with that part of the world which is other than me. Even while I am rationalizing, deceiving myself or having fantasies, I know that what is real is that I am dreaming.)

10. Love: "As an adult I can choose to meet, confront, witness, understand and be mirrored by another. I can also choose to love him and care for him." (Encounter)

(Explanation: I am capable of loving like an adult. I can love spiritually and I can love physically. I do not use love neurotically. In love I can accept the dignity and the needs of my partner in love. If I so choose, I am able to make love the central project in my life. I enjoy spiritual, emotional and physical love and love is easy and natural for me.)

11. Adaptability: "I choose myself as one who is realistically flexible." (Flexibility)

(Explanation: I can be reflective and inward or active and outgoing, depending on my own choices and the circumstances in which I find myself. I can be self-reliant and independent if I want to and have to, but I also can be dependent and trusting if I choose that personality structure. I can be both a leader and a follower, as my decisions and the world's circumstances dictate.)

12. **Time: "I experience time as living in a present which, while utilizing the past, connects directly and primarily into my future." (Futurity)**

(Explanation: I experience my life as a continuous progression. My sense of time is not fragmented. My focus is on the future. I live in the present and I realize that both past and future are connected to me in the present. The burdens of the past exist for me in the present. The hopes and opportunities for the future exist for me in the present. I experience the time of my life as a river that flows always and smoothly in the direction of the future.)

13. **Growth: "My life is an endless process of growing, emerging and reaching out." (Self-transcendence)**

(Explanation: For me, to live is to grow. I am not satisfied with achievements in life. My concern is rather with process and movement in my life. The meaning of my life is found in continual growth: in education, in human relationships, in occupational progress, in creativity, in building, etc. I feel that if my growing should end so would the meaning of my life. I know that hate and disinterest are the results of a reaching out that has been frustrated.)

14. **Contradiction: "The inescapable ambiguities and contradictions of life are my powerful allies." (Polarity, Dialectic)**

(Explanation: When faced with contradictions in life I am not upset; instead, I am challenged. I realize that values and situations are usually ambiguous and unclear. There are many sides to most issues. I feel no compulsion to discover always the absolute right. I can act in spite of uncertainty. I can make decisions in spite of ambiguities. I can make commitments without being certain of the truth. I can tolerate disagreement, opposition, rejection and denial. In fact, contradictions are to me a source of strength, since I find polarities within myself. I can integrate the polar opposites in me and achieve a mature sense of wholeness.)

APPENDIX B
Existential Sexuality Test

Score yourself according to the following set of "correct" answers. The rationale for the answers is given in Chapters 9–12, inclusive.

These questions should be marked T or A: 3–5, 7–9, 12, 13, 15, 18, 19, 22, 24, 30, 38, 39, 46, 56, 57, 61, 62, 66, 68, 71, 72, 74, 75, 79, 85.

These questions should be marked F or B: 1, 2, 6, 10, 11, 14, 16, 17, 20, 21, 23, 25–29, 31–37, 40–45, 47–55, 58–60, 63–65, 67, 69, 70, 73, 76–78, 80–84, 86, 87.

Make a checkmark before each question you answered *correctly*. Add the number of your checkmarks. That total is your final score.

Interpret your score according to the scale below. You are measuring the extent to which you manifest in your life a successful commitment to existential sexuality.

The scores are based on testing thirty-one students (thirteen men and eighteen women) in an upper-division summer university course.

NUMERICAL SCORE		MEANING (men and women combined)
72		far above average
65		above average
59		average
52		below average
46		far below average

The average for men was fifty-five, for women it was sixty-one.

Index